MARLENE '86

DISTRIBUTORS

PAUL H. CROMPTON LTD.
638 Fulham Road
London SW6, England

MARTIAL ARTS SUPPLY COMPANY
P.O. Box 5139
Durban 4000
Natal, Republic of South Africa

ZEN MARTIAL ARTS SUPPLY
P.O. Box 198
Gladesville, Sydney
N.S.W. 211, Australia

SPORT RHODE
6072 Dereieigh Spendlingen
Frankfurter Str. 121
West Germany

MARTIAL ARTS SUPPLIES
P.O. Box 6495
Te Aro, Wellington
New Zealand

BLACK BELT MARTIAL ARTS SUPPLY
19 John Street North
Hamilton, Ontario
Canada   L8R 1H1

KINJI SAN IMPORTS
3010 Avenue M
Brooklyn, N.Y.
11210

KATA BOOK SERVICE
P.O. Box 93189
Los Angeles, California
90093

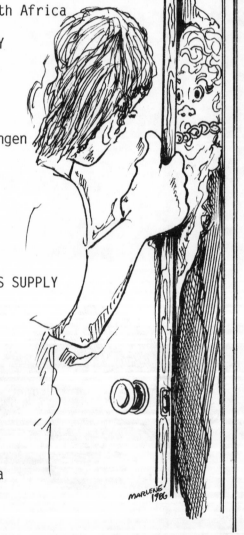

PRINTING   -WING KING TONG COMPANY LTD.
                 41-55 Wo Tong Tsui Street
                 3/f Eing Foo Industrial Bldg.
                 Kwai Chung, N.T.
                 Kowloon, Hong Kong

PUBLISHER   -MASTERS PUBLICATION
                 Hamilton, Ontario, Canada

PHOTOGRAPHERS   -Cyril Sharp
                 Branko Galic

COPY RIGHT 1986

ISBN 0-920129-12-9

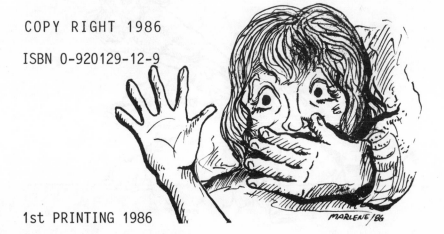

1st PRINTING 1986

Special thanks to Max and Judy for their undaunted support and continued encouragement throughout this endeavour.

FREEDOM FROM FEAR

by Bill Daniels & Sharon van Dyk

FREEDOM FROM FEAR

by Bill Daniels & Sharon van Dyk

GRAPHIC DESIGN - Annette Hellingrath

ISBN 0-920129-12-9

Illustrations by MARLENE SHORTT

MASTERS Publication
a division of
JAPANESE KARATE ACADEMY LIMITED
1109 Main Street East, Hamilton, Ontario
Canada L8M 1N9

PRINTED IN HONG KONG

Acknowledgement

We wish to thank the following people for their words of wisdom and vast experience.

Linda Thompson of the North Bay Rape Crisis Center, Randal B. LaMorre, B.A. Family Life and Sex Education Consultant. Also Sgt. H. Brennon of Belleville for 'Women .Alone' a public service pamphlet for women.

Susan Brownmiller 'Against Our Will' 1975, the Honourable Robert Welch, Q.C., Provincial Secretariat for Justice; 'Information for the victims of sexual assault'.

The Minister of Justice and Attorney General of Canada, also, James E. Berry, Sheila A. Berry, Max W. van Dyk, Payne Business Machines and our students Barbara Pattison, Tara van Dyk, Donna Douglas and all the dedicated students of self defense that earn their 'Freedom From Fear'.

Dedication

This book is dedicated to Donna, Katherine, Tammy and Tara.

Foreword

The education that you have earned, the secure
family life you have created for yourself, or the
life style you enjoy, could be burglarized like a
cheap chest of drawers and ripped from you by a
rapist. A rapist, who, for reasons unkown, chose
you as his victim. If the assault is **severe**
enough, those things you do to give your life
meaning and for which you are respected could be
lost forever.

Consider the following.

It is five o'clock Friday evening, the beginning of
Jane's weekend. It has been a particularly
productive week for her, one in which she easily
completed all of her assigned tasks. Jane decides
to reward herself. A quiet dinner with friends, a
movie, then a few drinks at her favourite pub.

There is nothing new about the routine and its
familiarity gives Jane a sense of well being. Time
taken to look good before she meets with her
friends compounds these feelings. Jane is
pleasantly flattered by attention she receives from
one man who offeres to buy her a drink. That kind
of socializing is not part of her plans for this
evening so she turns the man down as gently as
possible being careful not to insult or encourage
him.

At the end of the relaxing evening Jane leaves for her car in the parking lot behind the pub. She is parked at the far end of the lot under some trees.

Suddenly her path is blocked by the man who offered to buy her a drink earlier. He stands menacingly before her. His eyes tell Jane everything. A rush of adrenalin surges up to her face as the man grabes for her throat --- Jane stubles back --- too late, the man has caught her by the wrist. Jane screams. In blind fear she slaps at her attacker with her free hand, screaming. The man tightens his grip and slaps her hard on the side of her head. The slap stunnes Jane into silence. Janes's attacker hurles her to the ground tearing visciously at her clothing. He glares into Jane's eyes and threatens to kill her if she doesn't co-operate. Her screams of rape are ignored, then muffled by the man's hand. Jane's attempts to get away are futile. The more she struggles the more determined her attacker becomes and the more determined he becomes the more helpless Jane feels.

What the final outcome of such an attack would be is anyone's guess. It could depend on a number of circumstances, (1) where the rape takes place; (2) if someone comes to your aid; (3) the mental stability of your attacker, and (4) your ability to defend yourself.

Without any way of defending yourself, or knowledge of how to cope during such a crisis chances are good you will fail. In failing what would you lose? Your self dignity, you may have torn clothes or maybe you would just feel humiliated. If you are fortunate that is all you would lose. However the possibility strongly exists that you could be crippled for life, either mentally or physically or worse you could lose your life.

This fictionalized rape may not be all that fictional. Similar attacks can, and do occur across Canada, approximately every half hour of every day. An attack can take place any time of the day or night, or anywhere there is a woman. Most people are familiar with the report of a rape that occurred during daylight while a crowd not only watched, but cheered the rapist. Reports also tell us more that eighty five per cent of all rapes occur right in the victim's own neighbourhood. Many agencies and all police departments continually endeavour to educate women of existing dangers in the hope of preventing rape before it happens. In spite of this tireless effort, rapes continue as a very real danger. Regardless of who they are, or their age, rape is a high priority fear in women.

To begin to understand what must be done by you to safeguard yourself, begin by examining a few of the normal pitfalls some women fall into when it comes to their own protection. How often have you, for example, discussed with your friend, what you would do, if alone and suddenly confronted by a rapist? Such conversations can offer as many answers as there are people asking the question. In spite of this wide divergence, there is one underlying sense of unity. That unity is total disdain for any male who would assault a woman. Almost to the person, women would like to strike back at an attacker and slam him into a vulnerable position. They would like to hurt their attacker so badly, he would be reluctant to mount an assault on another woman. Few will deny, under the circumstances such thinking is completely justified.

Sadly, such a reaction is pure speculation, or merely gossiping about how to protect yourself. This verbalizing is not only making a promise to yourself you may not be able to keep, but it could be deadly dangerouus.

If I, for example, want to play on one of the local sport teams and my only commitment to that sport is to think about it, or verbalize my involvement, the probability of my playing on that team is virtually non-existant. Emotion is not enough to allow me to physically perform the skills required for that sport. If I practice that sport however, my chances of playing on that team are as good as anyone's. There is no difference in self defense. Talking about what one might consider doing is not self defense technique.

In other instances, some women look to their husband, brother, father or boyfriend for protection. Under this umbrella, some women feel safe. Unfortunately, the umbrella isn't always there. One young girl with a very powerful father and athletic brothers was raped right in her own home. The umbrella had gone out for the evening. Some women who live alone display a foolish hardiness in justifying independence with an attitude of false bravado.

There are many 'home made' solutions. Using common sense and honesty, you can discover how other women feel about 'home made' solutions. Begin by looking at your own concepts of self defense for yourself. You may be shocked to discover most women feel as you do and carry the same fear with them at all times. You can do something about that. Don't be like the guy with faulty brakes on his car who kept promising himself to take the car to the shop for repair. An emergency, which he believed would never happen, happened. He doesn't have to worry about his brakes any more.

CONTENTS

ONE

The Rapist

How can you tell if a person is a rapist?

You can't!

Trained experts, individuals and rape crisis personnel all agree that there is no specific way to describe a rapist, nor is there any way to measure the social or economic background of a rapist. It is a generally accepted concept that a rapist may use a method of operation. This method of operation is divided into five stages. It must be understood before we go any further, all rapists do not necessarily use a method of operation. The following is designed as a guideline only, to make you aware. With this awareness, you can effectively avoid a situation before it has an opportunity to begin. The five stages in this method of operation are: visiual, verbal, physical, sexual and physical assault.

Visual

A rapist begins a hunt by looking for someone he feels is easy prey, not easy in terms of 'loose', but someone who, in the rapist's mind, appears weak or vulnerable. It is important to note here, a rapist does not always seek healthy or beautiful women as victims. He may go after children, the elderly, or the handicapped. Remember, the rapist

17

in this the visual stage, is in fact, hunting. He seeks an individual he believes qualifies and whom he believes could be easily preyed upon. There is little, if anything, concrete you can do and it is quite possible you won't even be aware you are being stalked. At this stage the rapist can't be sure his observation is reliable, so he must make a move to substantiate that observation.

Verbal

Once the rapist has gained enough confidence in his observation, he will move on to the next stage. In this stage he will attempt to make verbal contact with you. This can be done in the most innocent of ways, such as asking you for a light, to a more complicated verbal attack, such as starting an argument. Whatever his approach, the rapist is still stalking you, looking for signs of weakness. He is trying to learn if he can control you. If you back down from an argument, it may indicate to him, he has in fact, made a good choice. If, at this point, you are able to convince him, you are not weak or vulnerable, his pursuit may go no further. Be careful not to anger him by insulting him in front of others and definately, don't get 'mouthy' or 'cocky'. Be firm and matter of fact. At this stage, you may just embarrass him and he may not care if he considers you an easy victim or not. He may seek vengence for his embarrassment and set out to hurt you as badly as he can. Never threaten anything you can't carry out and never, never tell anybody what you might do to them because you have self defense training. This is telling the rapist too much and may alert him to be careful and effectively destroy any element of surprise you have.

Understand, that when a rapist approaches you, he is looking for as little resistance as possible. He is seeking, at least in his mind, co-operation. He seeks control of you. You must prevent him from gaining that control. The rapist must be made to realize, control of you is not possible without a tremendous struggle. If he does feel he has gained essential control, he moves on to his next stage.

Physical

This is the stage where our rapist meets Jane, our fictional character, in the parking lot. You will recall how the man seemed to come out of nowhere. Eye contact was made and there was no doubt in Jane's mind as to what his intentions were. Jane displayed what is often referred to as a sixth sense, or as some people say, a gut feeling. If you listen to this gut feeling, or sixth sense, it can sometimes alert you to danger. At this stage, the rapist may display a weapon, or, as in Jane's case, threaten her with her life. As the rapist sought verbal control he now seeks physical control. It is important to him that he be able to gain control of his victim completely. His need is to have his victim as helpless as possible. This will allow him to do whatever he desires with his victim.

There is only one thing to do at this stage if you want to get away and that is to fight. If you know how to fight, or have training in self defense, you stay as calm as possible under the circumstances. Your chances of getting away are far greater than if you don't know how to fight, or don't have any defense in such a situation. If you don't know how to defend yourself, you could get lucky, but in all probability you are his for the taking. You would be in the same situation as the guy in the foreword who kept putting off getting his brakes fixed. You would be in a head on collision and as badly as you wanted to stop, the brakes won't be there. The rapist will be confident to move on to the next stage.

Sexual

Confidence of the rapist is at its peak. He has made his assessment of you. Verbal contact was made and he has moved into the physical contact stage by grabbing and threatening you. At this stage, you have three options.

Submit!

One is to submit. Submission means accepting the consequences and the consequences could be forced oral sex, forced sexual intercourse, sodomy, a beating or whatever the rapist may feel like doing. In one instance a rapist, an acknowledged rapist, (which will be covered later in this chapter) held a woman against her will in a motel room for over five hours. He did everything imaginable, including ramming a broom handle into her vagina. Yet, he never performed sexual intercourse with her. In deciding to submit, it is important to realize as many as eighty five per cent of all rapists never reach a climax. This is indicative that rape is a violent crime of punishment, not passion.

If you decide not to submit, you can do something unexpected, which is your element of surprise. Some women act mentally ill, others physically ill to the point of regurgetation. Do anything that will turn your rapist away from you. A rapist needs control of his victim and by usurping that control, he could lose interest or confidence in you and his desire to rape you. Doing something completely unexpected can be enough for him to think of you as unacceptable for his purpose. If you are trained in self defense, this can present a marvelous opportunity for you to execute a devastating technique, one which can send your attacker to the ground with great pain. Then, without hesitation you can run. Certainly, this requires practice and a calm presence of mind, but if you practice and keep your head, you can face your attacker and call a halt to the assault. If you don't practice, we relate back to the guy with faulty brakes.

Passive Resistance

Your second option is that of passive resistance, again, bringing in your element of surprise. Your object will be to catch your attacker off guard and administer a crippling blow. This will do two things if executed properly. First, it will change the situation around so you have control and secondly, it will disable the rapist. His response will be directed towards his own pain, allowing you to run away if the opportunity presents itself, or administer a final blow so you can get away.

You must administer the technique with as much force and determination as is possible. Your objective is to win, not just warn the rapist. A half hearted attempt will only encourage or anger your attacker and convince him you are the right choice. Your feeble attempt to gain your freedom can also signal the rapist you are trained and he will be more cautious. You have destroyed your element of surprise. You can be certain the rapist will not make a half hearted attempt at raping you.

Fight Back

Your third option is to fight back, right from the beginning, no holding back and determined you will not lose. You will be determined to neutralize your attacker. Attack him with as much force as you know he will use to attack you and you must do it with intensity and determination. Be realistic, if your attacker is six foot four inches and weighs two hundred and fourty pounds and you are five foot two inches and weigh one hundred and ten pounds, don't try to punch it out with the guy. You won't be using common sense and you'll probably lose the battle and lose badly. Most men don't stand much of a chance against a big guy like that. You must be smarter than he is. Go for vulnerable areas as soon as they are visable to you --- be determined to win.

Physical Assault

In realistic terms, we have to look at the possibility you did not succeed in your bid to get away. The rapist has succeeded and penetration was forced on you. This can be the most dangerous time of the five stages. You have no idea what your

21

attacker might do next. Will he continue the assault or will he just go away? There is no way to know. It is no longer a matter of a few bruises and lacerations, it could be life or death. The rapist could decide to continue his assault on you, rid the area of evidence or he may decide to dispose of you. There really are no options left for you. You must fight back. Mentally, you must not be afraid to hurt your attacker or get hurt yourself. You must use anything at your disposal; a rock, a stick, an ash tray, kick, bite, scratch, anything. You must go for vulnerable areas with a vengeance and exert as much force and aggression as is humanly possible for you. At this stage, you only have one thing to concern yourself with, that is to live.

Blitz and Acknowledged Rapes

Keep in mind, our fictionalized rape of Jane, isn't the only way rape occurs. Women aren't raped only by strangers. Seventy percent of rape victims are known by the rapist. It is estimated only ten percent of all rapes are reported.

Care has been taken to make sure nobody is going to accept as gospel the five stages of rape for all rape cases. Proof that the five stages are not the only way a rape occurs lies in the 'blitz' rape and the 'acknowledged' rape. The blitz rape is not pre-meditated. This kind of rape is called an impulse rape, be it drug related or burglary related. If a woman stumbles on a burglar, he may, on impulse, decide to rape the intruder. The attack is quick. The burglar wants to complete his attack and get out. The object of the blitz rape is to gratify the burglar's desires through criminal acts, because of sexual fantasies or sexual perversion. If to kill is part of that perversion the blitz rapist can kill.

There is, in some instances of blitz rape, little regard for human life. Talking, pleading, or crying may prove useless against such an attacker. Some of these blitz rapists may not be in touch with their feelings and it can be impossible to communicate with them. If you are trained, you can strike quickly, but you must injure a blitz rapist severely, particularly if you suspect drugs are involved. You must have as little regard for him as he will have for you.

An acknowledged rape involves the trust or confidence factor. The rapist can be a relative, friend, friend of a friend, next door neighbour, co-worker, lover, fiance or someone you date. Because the trust factor is involved, the victim can be maneuvered into a vulnerable situation. The sudden realizaion of what is happening may prevent an immediate response from you to fight back.

Often the victim of an acknowledged rape will not report the incident for fear of breaking up a family, destroying a friendship or even loss of a job. Guilt may play a role in the mind of the victim after the rape. Confusion can set in and the victim may wonder what she has done to encourage the rape and may begin to rationalize her own guilt. As pointed out earlier, seventy per cent of all rapes are acknowledged rapes. This does not mean all relatives, friends, etc., are rapists. It is wise to be aware of potential danger, but it is foolish to replace one fear with paranoia. Be aware, be very aware, but don't defeat the purpose of this book to gain your freedom by placing yourself in a prison of fear from everyone you think strange by your own standards.

Your greates defense against either of these types of rape is common sense. Do your utmost to avoid areas where you can be placed in a vulnerable position. If, for example, you know of a praticular parking lot that has been subjected to vandalism and thefts, avoid the parking lot even if it means walking an extra five minutes in a well lit area.

TWO

Training Outline

It has been said, advice can be worth less than a penny a bushel. If that is true, advising a person to remain calm during a physical attack can't be worth the stale air expelled to utter the advice. The same can not be said of common sense. No one can teach common sense. We all develop this sometimes elusive part of our personality through the process of time and maturity. Often, when a specific situation is explained to us, the common sense conditions surrounding the situation become immediately obvious. Common sense tells us there could be no other answer for that particular situation at least according to our experience.

When you seek reasons for a rapist's behaviour, there doesn't appear to be any common sense involved. The rapist's primary objective is not sex, but violence. Statistics bear this out. Sixty two per cent of the victims are physically injured in some way, while nine per cent of the victims are severely beaten. Common sense, if nothing else, tells you a rapist is serious. This same common sense, if put to use properly, can be a very effective weapon.

In using common sense, think of your hands and feet as tools for self defense. Understand, these same tools you use to protect yourself, are the same tools a rapist will use to attack you with. You will learn to use your own tools more effectively. You will be using stronger body parts against weaker body parts of the rapist. For example, a finger is much stronger than an eye, the forearm is stronger than the hand and shoulders are stronger than fingers.

There are a host of examples of common sense and the element of surprise as there are a host of examples of stronger body parts over weaker body parts. Begin to think of these things in terms of self defense. Ask yourself questions about male and female anatomy and what must take place before intercourse can begin, let alone be completed. Put these things into perspective when it comes to rape and forced sex. There are certain things a male must do before he can·perform the act. Think of these things in terms of self defense and seek times of vulnerability for the male and think in terms of self defense. When you are alone, visualize yourself defending against an attacker, be sure to visualize yourself defeating the attacker with your techniques. Do this while in bed, in the car, walking, at the supermarket, or anywhere at all.

For best results in learning the physical aspects of self defense, follow a routine. When possible, practice with a partner. An ideal situation would be to get someone you can practice with on a regular basis. You may even think of forming a group to practice with and make your sessions a time to discuss the fears or concerns you have. The objective is to learn as much about your own fears as you can and do something about them and also to learn as much as you can about a rapist.

If you have a partner who tries to be 'macho' and won't allow you to practice because he/she is trying to prove they are better and stronger than you, get another partner. You are not trying to prove which of you is better and stronger. Get another partner, you are not trying to satisfy anybody's ego. You want to learn how to defend yourself and in the beginning you are going to have to go slow and go through the motions slowly, until you understand how the technique works. If you don't have an immediate partner, practice in front of a mirror. Compare your technique with those in the photographs. A mirror can be an exellent way to perfect your technique.

Your training is broken down into four segments, tools, target areas for tools, combinations and weapons. The first thing is to learn what tools you have and how to use them. Once you have learned the tools available to you and how to use them, you will learn what areas of the body to hit. Following this, you will learn how to put these tools into a combination or series of strikes in sequence. The fourth part of your training consists of weapons. You will be taught a few very basic forms with the long stick.

In self defense nothing is definite. One technique may feel very comfortable to you and easy to execute, yet the same technique may feel awkward and difficult to execute for your partner. Experiment with yourself and with your partner. Discover what is good for you, what feels comfortable and powerful to you. If something is just physically impossible for you to perform, scrap it and go on to something else. But before you set aside any technique, give it a one hundred and ten per cent effort. You could eliminate a technique that could prove very effective for you in the long run.

Many of the techniques in the martial arts are difficult at first, but after dedicated practice they feel comfortable. The more you learn you may discover you can invent effective combinations of your own. The major point is, don't stop at this book or the techniques and combinations in it, continue to learn.

Begin your training slowly. There is a natural

tendency to execute your techniques too fast after only a few practice sessions. Don't be overly concerned with speed at the beginning. Let your speed develop with your ability to execute the techniques. We are all born with either fast twitch or slow twitch muscle fibre. Slow twitch fibres are for endurance, fast twitch fibres are for speed and strength. The ratio for fast twitch fibres and slow twitch fibres in the body is determined at birth. All of the exercising you do isn't going to change this fact, however, training will maximize the performance of these fibers. Concentrate on your technique. Your reflexes will improve through training, or at least they will peak.

Suggested Training Schedule

(1) Exercise and warm up before each training session. (2) Begin by practicing with your individual tools, for example finger strikes. Do this in repetitions. A repetition is the number of times you perform the exercise or technique. The number of repetitions is done in sets which means you would do 10 repetitions and then rest. That would constitute one set. Then do another 10 repetitions or set. To do your finger strikes you would form the finger as shown in the photograph in the next chapter. Relax, then form it again for 10 repetitions. When you are finished with the right hand, do the left. Do the same for each tool. Establish a number of sets and repetitions you find comfortable for your own personal routine. You may find, if you are right handed, that the left handed techniques are awkward. This is normal. The solution is to perform more repetitions with your left hand than with your right hand.

(3) When you have completed the above, get your partner and go on to the use of your tools to vulnerable areas. Practice each one individually as above. Decide your own number of sets and repetitions. (4) Combinations are next. This is

where you begin to understand the importance of using your tools correctly and to perform each technique as perfectly as possible. You may feel that there is little power in your combinations to begin but this is where your practice comes into play. It is important for you to understand that a great deal of practice on your part is necessary for you to perfect these combinations with effective power.

It is strongly suggested in your scheduling that you begin by spending most of your practice time on individual tools and striking areas. As you feel more comfortable with the individual tools and striking areas, increase your time for these areas and increase your time for your combinations. Continue to spend time on your basics. They can always be improved, no matter how long or often you practice them. (5) There is no secret to using weapons. The only requirement is the same dedication you plan on applying to your regular schedule.

THREE

Conditioning

The importance of conditioning for self defense, or any other physical activity can not be overemphasized. It can mean the difference between winning or losing. Your ability to execute techniques will be in direct proportion to the amount of time spent practicing and perfecting your techniques. A list of twelve suggestions to keep in mind while training is followed by fourteen exercises. The exercises will not only contribute to your conditioning but will assist in the execution of your techniques.

(1)   Warm up before beginning any training program.
(2)   If possible, exercise the same time every day.
(3)   Never exercise to the point of extreme exhaustion.
(4)   If you begin to wheeze during exercises, stop at once.
(5)   Try not to allow more than ninety-six hours to pass between exercise sessions. Experts tell us that after ninety-six hours the benefit of the workout begins to deteriorate.
(6)   Exercise at least three times a week.
(7)   Listen to your body. Some days a light workout will be sufficient because your body is tired.
(8)   Set up a training schedule.
(9)   Increase your exercising program sensibly. Take your time and do it right.

31

(10) Plan on beginning a running program, begin in terms of minutes, not distance.
(11) Allow yourself time to cool down after each training session.
(12) Fitness Canada tells us that thirty minutes of exercising three times a week will keep us in shape.

EXERCISES

When you begin these exercises, do them slowly until you and your body get used to them.   Your greates gains will be made by doing the exercises correctly and remember, it takes time to get into shape.   Use common sense to dictate when to increase the number of repetitions for each exercise.

RUNNING ON THE SPOT

This exercise is similar to jogging, except you stay in one spot. Hold your hands in a fighting position, running on the balls of your feet. Perform this exercise in terms of time, rather than repetitions. Run as fast as you can, lifting your knees as high as you can. While performing the exercise, look around. This will help you to be aware of your surroundings while performing a physical activity.

NECK EXERCISE

Roll your head slowly from left to right, allowing your head to make a complete circle. Keep your eyes open at all times. If you do this exercise too quickly, you may get dizzy. When you have completed your repetitions, left to right, do the exercise right to left. When you have completed the above exercises, place your chin on your chest then bring your head back until you are looking up at the ceiling. Return your chin to your chest and repeat the exercise.

WAIST TWIST

Place both hands on your hips, twist only the upper part of your body from your trunk. Your feet are spread approximately shoulder width. Twist from side to side.

TOUCH TOES

Legs spread as wide as possible, knees slightly bent, place your right hand on your left foot, bringing your left arm straight over your head as shown. Bring your left hand down to your right arm over your head. Perform the exercise slowly to begin. Increase the speed as you become more comfortable with the exercise.

PUSH UPS

Lying on your stomach, place your hands approximately shoulder width apart, at your shoulders. Keep your feet together. Push your upper body up with your arms until they are fully extended. Look straight ahead, keep your palms flat on the floor. As your arm strength increases, you may find it necessary to lift your whole body in full push up.

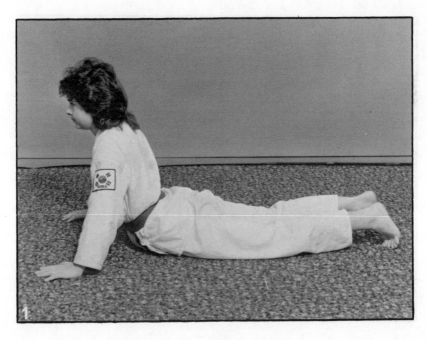

ELBOW TO FLOOR

Feet spread as wide as possible, knees slightly
bent, place your hands flat on the floor down from
your shoulders. Lower your body by bending the
elbows only. Touch your elbows to the floor then
push yourself back up to the starting position.
This is not a strength exercise, but a stretching
exercise. You should feel a pull on your inner
thigh.

HEAD TO FLOOR

Same postion as previous page. This time grab your ankles and bend at the waist touching your head to the floor.

HEAD TO KNEE

Still in the same postion grab your ankle with both hands and touch your head to your knee. When completed, repeat on the other side.

LEG STRETCHES

Lying flat on the floor, lift your right leg straight up, keeping your foot parallel with the ceiling. There should be a pulling on the back of your leg. When you have completed your repetitions, repeat with you left leg.

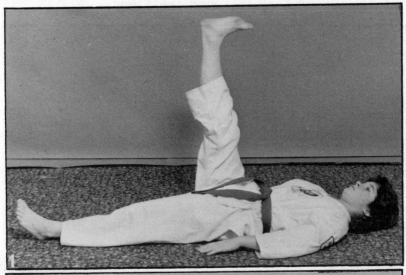

V SITS

Sit on the floor as shown in the photograph, placing your hands flat on the floor and under your hips. Raise your feet six inches from the floor then swing both feet out to the side. Hold, then slowly return to starting position. Repeat and do not allow your feet to touch the floor.

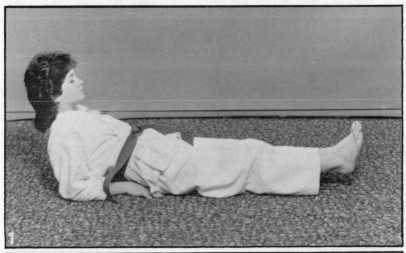

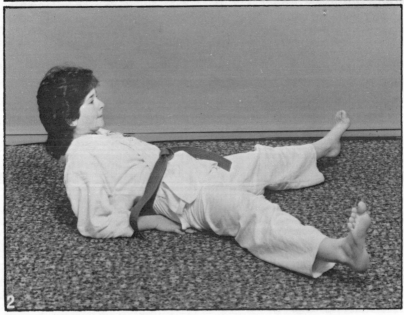

HALF SQUATS

LEG SWINGS

Place a chair behind you. Fold your arms in front of you across your chest. Lower your body with only leg strength until your buttocks barely touches the chair. Don't allow yourself to sit. As soon as your buttocks touches the chair, lift yourself up with your legs only.

LEG SWINGS

This is a balancing exercise. Stand on one leg, knee slightly bent and swing your leg up and back without touching the floor.

FRONT KICK

Stand as in the photograph, right leg behind you.
Bring your left knee forward and up, as high as
possible. Use your knee like the site of a gun,
where you point your knee is where your foot will
strike. Snap your foot out toward your target then
bring your foot back as quick or quicker than you
kicked out. (This prevents an attacker from
grabbing your foot.) Set your foot back to the
starting position. There are four moves to this
kick and the idea is to develop a rhythm. Knee is
brought up, kick out at target, return leg quickly
and return to the starting postition. When you are
practicing this front kick, count as you kick to
develop a rhythm.

SIDE KICK

Lift your leg to the side, then shoot your foot out at the target. Return your foot to the original positon, step down and repeat. This kick is designed for the lower areas of the body such as the knees or toes.

PALM HEEL THRUST

For the palm heel explanation see Chapter 4.

FOUR

Tools

Everything you have read to this point has dealt with the mental process of defending yourself. There is the understanding of common sense and the element of surprise as an integral part of any person's self defense, which in itself is not enough. There is a need to add outward action, an action physically backing up your thought process. This mental process must now be joined with your physical tools. The singular component that will separate you from 'home made' solutions, is you will no longer just 'think' about what you would like to be able to do, you will be able to do it. When you are practicing with your tools of self defense, you must concentrate very hard, in fact you must discipline yourself to a point where outside noises will not interrupt your training.

The more you concentrate, the more intense you will become in executing your techniques. When you realize your concentration and intensity are very strong, speed up your routines. You must increase your concentration and intensity, giving yourself confidence to strike with a vengeance plus power and speed.

The physical tools you will use to accomplish this confidence are your fingers, palm heel, elbow, hammer fist, knee and foot. The tools are directed to vulnerable areas. There are four major striking areas and nine minor striking areas. The major areas are the eyes, throat, groin and the knee. The minor striking areas are the toes, shin, small ribs, nose, under the nose, kidneys, spine, neck and temple.

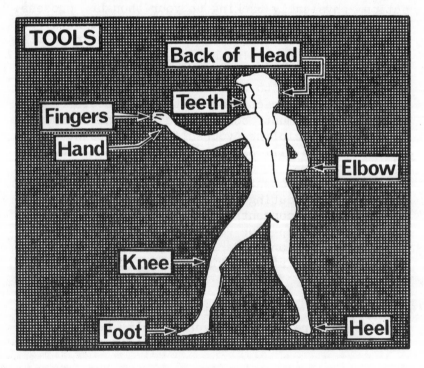

FINGER

Press your thumb against the second knuckle of your index finger and at the same time, press the second knuckle of your middle finger against the second knuckle of your index finger. Bend your index finger slightly as shown in the photograph. If you keep your finger straight and stiff, it could bend backward upon impact and easily break. Press your thumb hard against your index finger while pressing your remaining fingers hard against the index finger. Stiffen your slightly bent striking finger. A two finger strike is executed the same way using right and left fingers formed as shown.

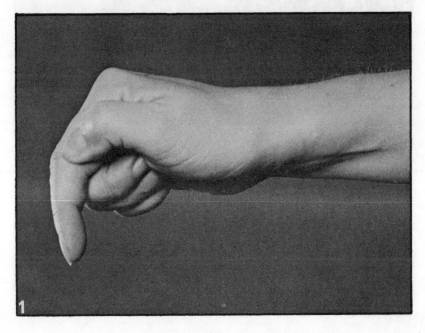

FIST

To make a fist, follow the photographs. Before you place your thumb over your knuckles, squeeze your fingers tight and curl them into your palm as snugly as you can. When you bring your thumb over your fingers, make a fist as tight as you can.

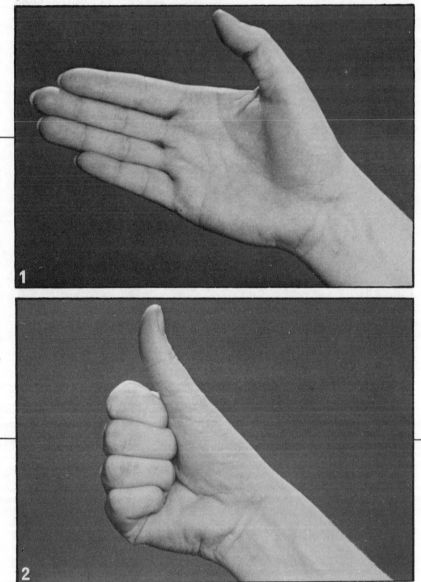

PALM HEEL

To show a photograph of the action of the palm heel proved fruitless. It was decided an explanation would better suit the purpose and be less confusing. Begin by holding your hand at shoulder level, palm down. Keep your hand and wrist loose, even limp. When you execute a strike, make sure your hand lines up with the centre of your body. Strike out with your palm heel, directing your palm to the target. At the last second, before impact, drop your wrist down and at the same time, snap your hand back. Dropping of the wrist and snapping action of the hand are critical in this technique. When you learn to time this technique perfectly, you will have a wonderful weapon. It will feel right when you do it right.

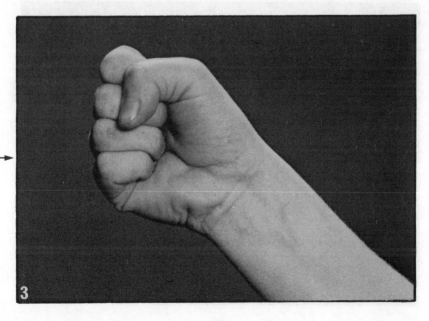

V FINGER

Your thumb is placed on the second knuckle of your third finger as shown in the photograph. Stiffen your striking fingers, keeping them slightly bent. At the same time, press hard against your knuckle, tightening your entire hand as well as your fingers.

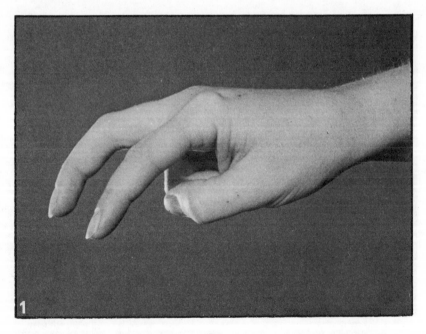

ELBOW

Palm up, hand about halfway up your wrist. You are striking with the elbow and must thrust the striking part of your elbow toward your target. As your elbow moves toward the target, your palm twists toward the floor. Impact on the target area and twisting of the palm downward must be co-ordinated. Impact and palm down happen simultaneously.

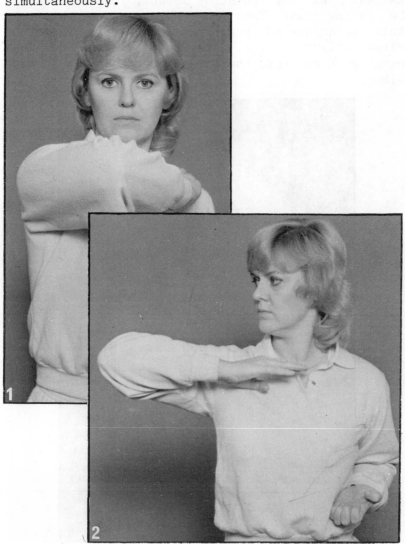

BLOCKING
HIGH BLOCK

Your block has to develop speed, as if you were
punching. Begin by making a fist and make your
fist as tight as you can. Hold your fist at your
side, palm up, about halfway up your rib cage.
Punch upward. As you punch upward, your fist
twists. At the point of impact, your fist should
be facing away from you. When you are practicing
this technique and punching into the air, keep your
elbow slightly bent. To fully extend your elbow
when puching into the air can cause damage to your
elbow.

BLOCKING
MIDDLE BLOCK

Again, make a fist as tight as you can and hold your arm halfway up your rib cage. Snap your arm out in front of you and slightly to the side as shown in the photograph. Snap your arm toward the attacking tool. This too, is a punching action, but you are punching shorter than the high block. Direct your blocking tool to the inside arm of the attacking tool to drive it away from you and at the same time opening a possible striking area.

BLOCKING
LOW BLOCK

Again make a tight fist and hold it halfway up your rib cage. Punch downward to the inside of the striking tool. When you make contact your palm will be down. Be careful not to hit with your knuckles. This could cause a lot of pain and damage to you. This block can also be used against kicks, but you must be extrememly cautious blocking a kick. The wisest response when you are kicked at is to get out of the way, however, if you are not in a position to do so you can use this block. Be extremely cautious about punching a leg with your fist, you could break your hand.

HEEL

The heel can be used in the side kick or for stomping. For stomping on toes drive your heel into the rapist's toes as shown, or use a side kick to kick out and drive your heel into your attacker's knee from the side.

In executing any of the kicks or strikes, punch or kick right through your attacker. For example, if you were to administer a palm heel to the nose, sight through your attacker's nose, right to the back of his head. If you are driving a knee into your attacker's knee, drive it through to a point beyond his knee.

KNEE

There is little distance between a knee and the groin area. The knee can be a very effective weapon and can be executed without your attacker even knowing it if he is holding you against his body. When you use your knee, lift from the hips, not the foot. By using your hip you can get your body weight behind the impact.

FOOT

Bring your knee up as in executing a knee, then snap your foot toward your target, using the instep. To practice your kick, do it in four stages.

(1) Right leg is back. (2) Snap your foot toward the target. (3) Return your foot to the knee position. Do this as fast or faster than you kicked out to prevent your attacker from grabbing your foot if you were to just let it hang. (4) Return to the original position. Practice slowly until you gain balance. Keep your support leg slightly bent for balance.

63

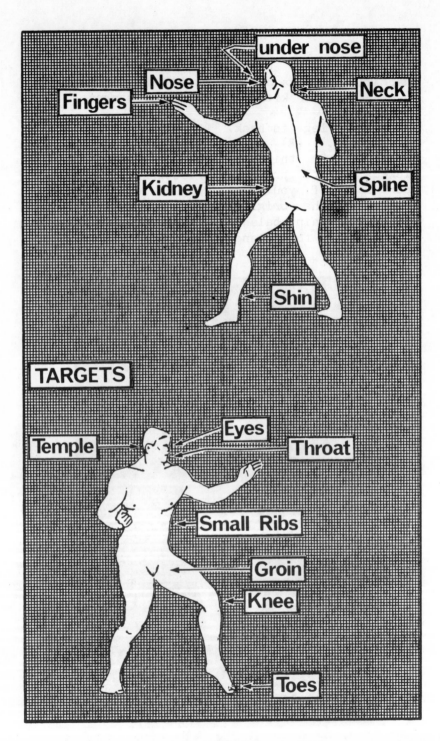

FIVE

Targets

The preceding chapter showed the relative simplicity of the tools you will be using for your own self defense. Where you strike with these tools will determine a major portion of the effectiveness of your element of surprise. You wouldn't try to disable a rapist with a finger strike to the thigh, nor would you elbow him on the arm. Your tools have to be delivered to specific areas. As you progress, you will discover for yourself what is sensible and effective for you.

FINGER STRIKE

Finger strikes go to the eyeball whether you are using a single finger, a double finger or a V finger strike. Practice each technique as shown with a partner. If you do not have a partner, practice using your mirror image. In some instances when an attacker has a firm hold on you at arms length, there is little he can do. If for instance he were to pull you in close you would knee him in the groin or execute a finger strike, or both. If he were to pull you in too fast and too close to execute either a finger strike or a knee just smash your head into his nose.

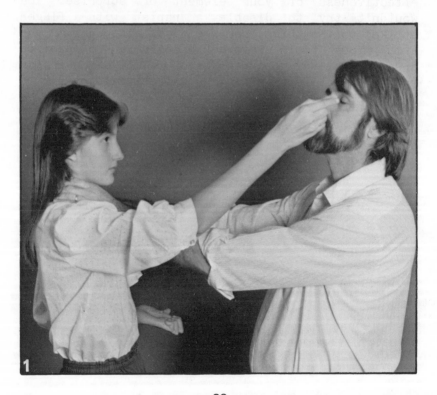

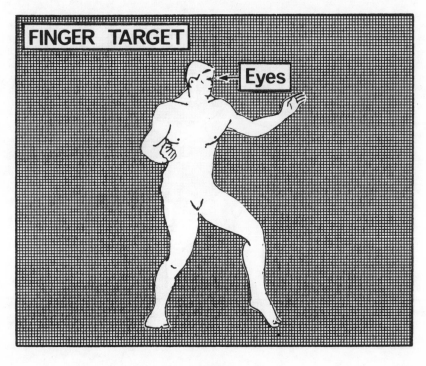

FINGER TARGET

Eyes

ELBOW

The elbow is administered to the chin, the jaw, the temple and the throat. The elbow can be a very effective tool and can also be driven into the eyes and the groin. Experiment with your elbow blows. Discover in which situations an elbow strike is possible, including tight spots like in a corner or in a car. Be sure to practice your elbow strikes as shown in a specific number of repetitions and sets.

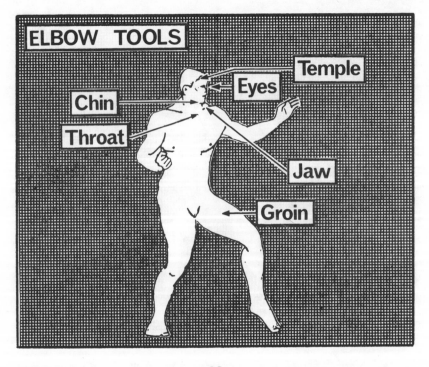

ELBOW TOOLS

Temple

Eyes

Chin

Throat

Jaw

Groin

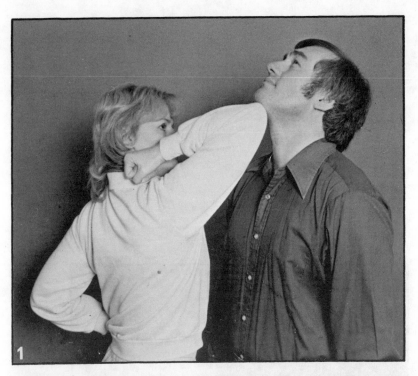

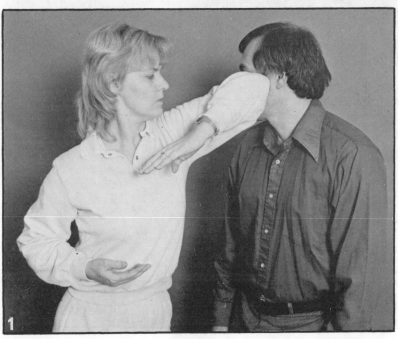

FOOT

Using your instep, kick to the groin of your partner, then practice kicking to the knee and shin. The hammer fist can also be executed to the nose, throat or eyes.

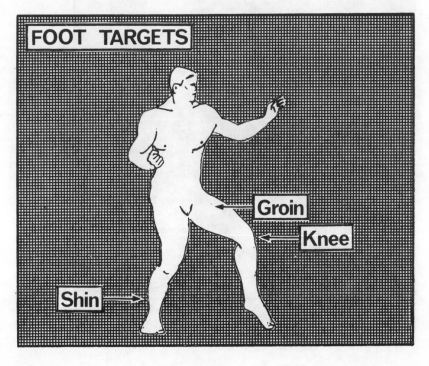

FOOT TARGETS

Groin

Knee

Shin

BLOCKING

Blocks don't need to strike a vulnerable area for your purpose of self defense. Other chapters will show you how to block and then counter with a strike. To practice the blocks, have your partner grab at you as shown.

PALM HEEL

Practice all of the palm heel strikes hitting the designated areas shown in the photographs. The palm heel is administered to the nose, the throat, the temple and the groin. Practice the palm heel thrust by yourself as often as you can while sitting watching television or having a cup of tea. Practice it until it feels right.

PALM HEEL TARGETS

Temple

Nose

Throat

Groin

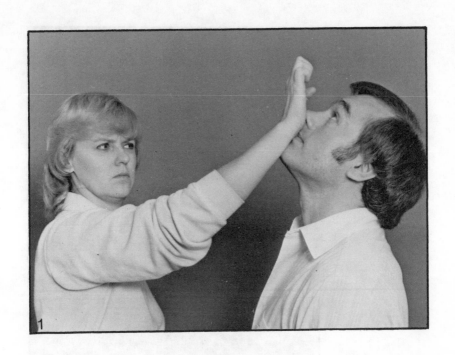

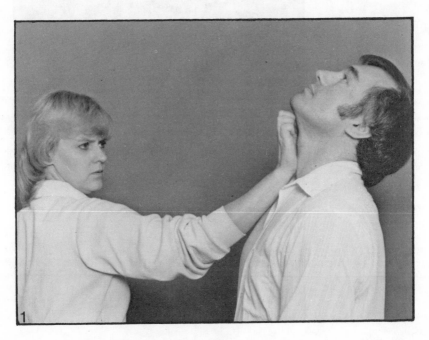

75

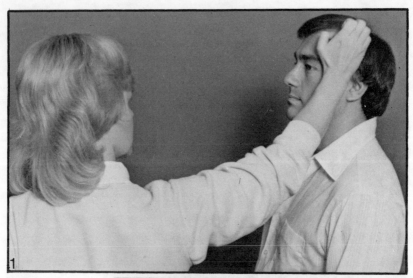

76

HEEL

Stomp to the toes and side kick to the knee. The stomp can also be executed to the spine, knee, groin, throat and head.

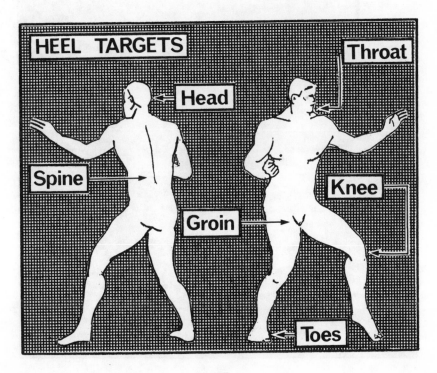

HEEL TARGETS

Throat

Head

Spine

Knee

Groin

Toes

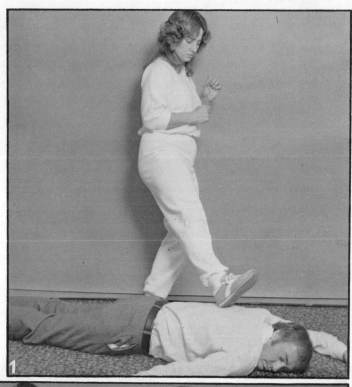

78

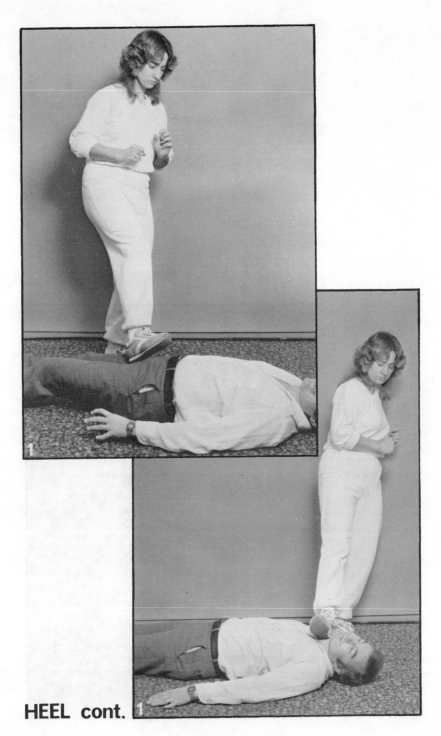

HEEL cont. 1

HEEL cont.

SIX

Releases

Kicking and punching are excellent self defense techniques, but in reality, in a situation which could mean the difference between life and death, they are simply not enough. During research through interviewing trained professionals such as policemen and security guards, they tell us the majority of fights feature three or four kicks or punches. Combatants will grab each other and begin grappling. When you relate back to our fictional character, Jane, her attacker reached for her throat then grabbed her by the arm. If at that stage, Jane had known how to get out of the arm grasp, the results of her attack may have been different.

In releasing from a grasp, you must pit stronger muscle parts against weaker muscle parts. For example, the forearm is stronger than the thumb and the shoulder is stronger than the hand.

When you have learned to release from the grip of an attacker by practicing the techniques, you can experiment and discover other means of releases. These releases are probably the most difficult part of your training, yet they are vital to you to have a well rounded self defense program. There is no secret to learning releases. As in other techniques, they require a great deal of concentration and practice. We will show you how to release yourself from the grip of a male attacker, even though that male is much stronger and more muscular than you are.

The two photographs on the opposite page show a stick half way out of the palm. The stick is used to demonstrate to you how you must stiffen your forearm from the elbow down to your finger tips. The forearm, as the stick shows, moves against the thumb. You twist your arm into the attacker's hand until the ulna bone, (the bone that runs parallel to your thumb), is between your attacker's thumb and index finger. Don't twist your forearm too much. Twist just enough to place the ulna bone into position. Twisting too far could place your forearm into the strength of your attacker's fingers.

PRACTICE WITH A STICK

To practice this technique have your partner hold a stick in your hand as shown in photo one. Very gently, have your partner move that stick between your thumb and index finger.

Slowly begin to practice the technique shown in photo two. The important part of learning these releases is to get the feel of the movement. When you feel that you have confidence in the technique, tighten your grip enough to make your partner work a little harder. A kick to the shins can be used to divert your attacker's attention prior to the release.

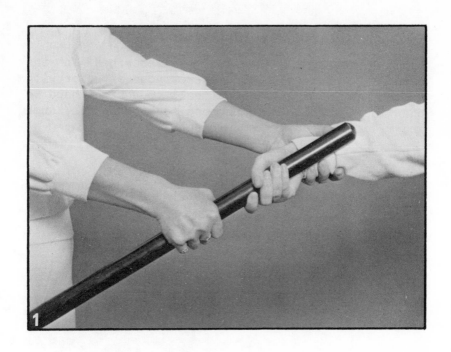

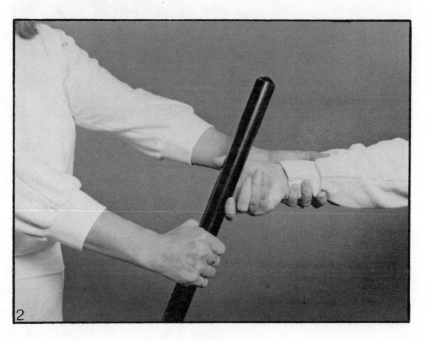

GRABBED RIGHT ON RIGHT

Using the same technique as described in the preceding photographs, distract your attacker with almost any technique and roll your right hand to the inside until the ulna bone is between his thumb and middle finger, then pull out.

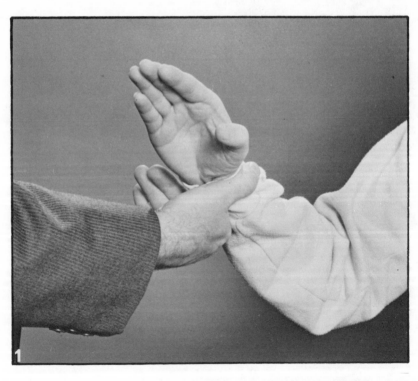

GRABBED RIGHT ON LEFT

Again distract your attacker with any technique and roll your left hand to the inside until the ulna bone is between his thumb and middle finger and pull out.

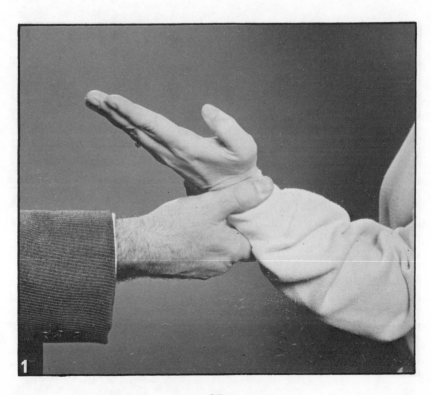

GRABBED BY TWO HANDS

Both your hands will go to the outside at the same time. Execute your distraction prior to your release.

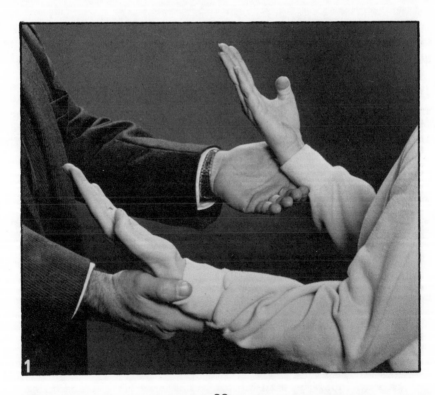

GRABBED TWO HANDS ON ONE

Reach between your attacker's two arms and grab your own hand. With your free hand, pull up between the thumbs. If your attacker has you the opposite way, reach down and through his arms and pull out against his thumbs. If his hands are reversed, with the thumbs at opposite sides, administer a good technique and pull the same way as before.

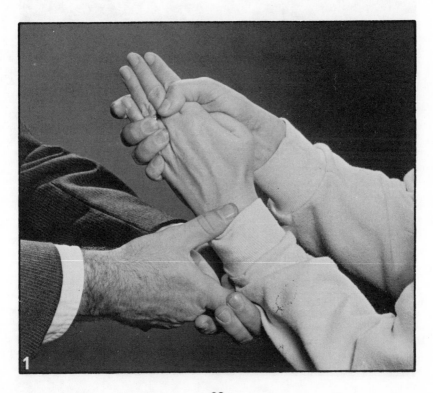

SEVEN

Single Technique

When you are grabbed by a strong person there is a tremendous feeling of helplessness. You feel trapped. To alleviate this helpless feeling, we will begin with a series of very simple one move self defense techniques. Practice each defense move until you feel comfortable with your escape. Replace the helpless feeling with one of confidence in your ability to ease yourself from a strong grasp.

DEFENSE 1

The attacker grabs you from behind in a hammer lock. The very first thing you do, is tuck your chin into the crook of his elbow as deep as you can. Touch your chin to your chest, if possible. This will prevent the attacker from cutting off your air supply. His method of attack may hurt for a few seconds, but if you react immediately, you will be able to breathe and won't panic. From this positon you can administer a hammer fist to the groin or a stomp to the toes.

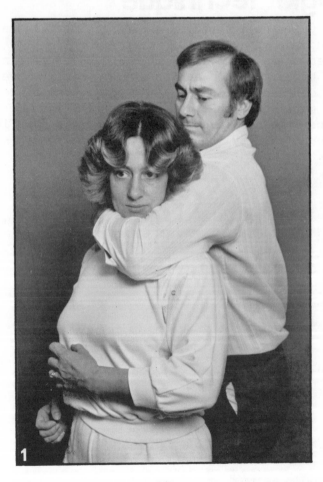

DEFENSE 2

You may be sitting in a theatre by yourself and someone you may be casually dating decides to place his hand on your knee to work his hand upwards. You may not wish that kind of intimacy but you don't want to seriously hurt your companion. Place your hand on his as though you don't really object to his advances. Turn your hand as you rub his hand, until your elbow is facing him. Grab a finger, any finger, and bend it back. Be careful doing this, unless you want to break his finger. If you do not wish to date him again, maybe you could decide to break his finger. If so, don't expect to be asked out again. If you wish to remain friends, just hurt him enough to let him know you wish him to keep his hands to himself.

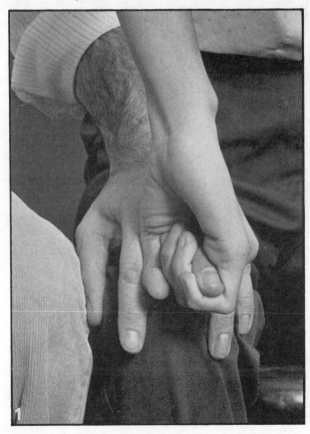

DEFENSE 3

Our victim is grabbed by the colar and jerked
forward. There is nothing she can do about the
attacker's strength. She can't change his strength
so her option is to use his strength against
himself. As he pulls her forward, she administers
a knee to the groin. Once the decision has been
made to administer this technique, do so with as
much force as possible and do not worry about
hurting your assailant. Your knee is stronger than
the testicles and the hit and run situation applies
here. As soon as contact has been made, run away.

DEFENSE 4

The attacker has our victim off her feet. The attacker can do nothing in this position unless he lets go. He has effectively tied himself up. He may try for a kiss but in this position that is all he can do. A good hard smash to his nose with your forehead will force him to let go. There may be blood and certainly tears will come to his eyes as a result of this self defense technique. If he has you off the ground from the rear, smash the back of your head into his nose. Again when he drops you, either finish him with a final blow as an area becomes visible or run away.

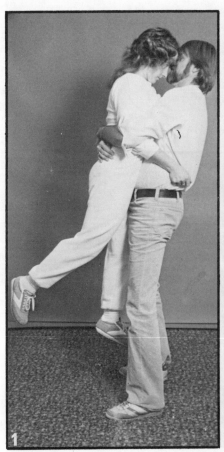

DEFENSE 5

The attacker is on top of the victim. At this
stage there is little the attacker can do.
Although the victim appears helpless, he has
effectively incapacitated his own hands. He may
try to kiss you, this is your chance. Act
responsive, then firmly grasp his bottom lip
between your teeth and rip it off. There will be
plenty of blood and it will be messy, but this will
more than likely send him into a state of shock and
enable you to make your escape.

DEFENSE 6

Some things just aren't worth fighting for.

EIGHT

Two Strike Techniques

The techniques in this chapter require more movement than one step. techniques. In this chapter, pay close attention to foot placement.

SELF DEFENSE 1

When grabbed by the throat as shown, attempting to release the grip by twisting and turning your head would likely prove futile. You must use a stronger body part other than the neck to free yourself. Use your shoulders as shown in the second photo. Twist your whole body with a jerk and step back slightly. If you twist in a cork screw manner (start twisting from your feet and up your body to your shoulders), your technique won't work. When twisting, twist as if you were moving only one side of your entire body with a quick jerking action.

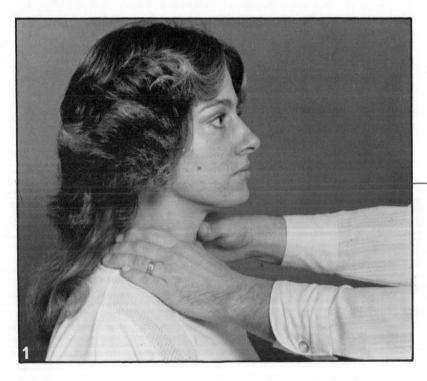

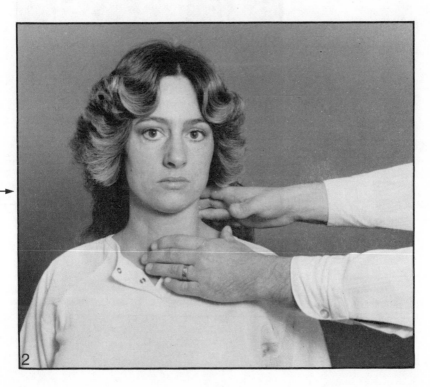

SELF DEFENSE 2

When grabbed by the shoulder, with one hand or two as in this photo, twist your entire body as in self defense number one except that you step back quickly. Keep your arm stiff and place it across your opponent's elbow as shown. It is absolutely necessary to contact your opponent's elbow in this technique to gain control.

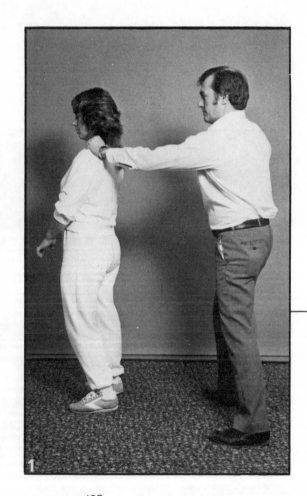

SELF DEFENSE 3

When grabbed by the hair, (notice the position of the victim's right leg), step in with your right leg and execute a knee strike to the groin.

SELF DEFENSE 4

This is an excellent technique which can be applied quickly and effectively when sitting in your car with little room to maneuver in. Make a hitchhiking thumb. As soon as your attacker relaxes because he feels you are going to co-operate, execute the thumb to the eye. If you feel that you can get out of the car and away, then do it. Run into a stranger's house if necessary. If you feel an added blow is needed, grab your attacker's hair and smash his nose into the dashboard of your car.

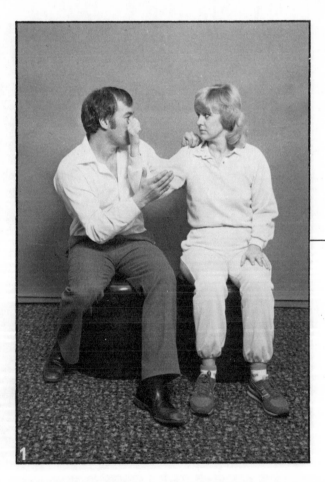

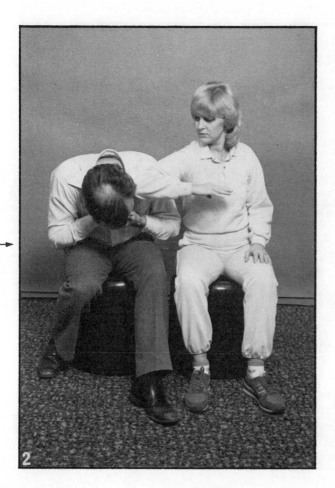

SELF DEFENSE 5

The attacker has grabbed you around the neck from behind. (Remember to tuck your chin into the crook of the attacker's elbow as shown in Chapter 7). Notice that in the next photo the victim has stepped to the outside of her attacker's right leg with her left leg, making it possible for her to execute a hammer fist to the attacker's groin.

SELF DEFENSE 6

You may get pushed to the ground. If you do, twist and turn as fast as you can to keep your attacker at your feet. If he moves in execute a side kick right through his knee. Before he recovers and if he is still within range as in the next photo, execute a side kick to his face. Get up as fast as you can and run.

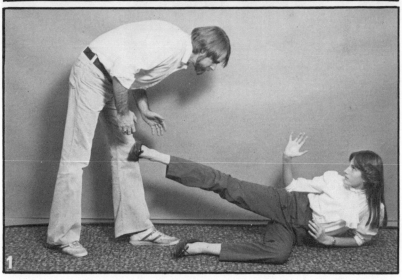

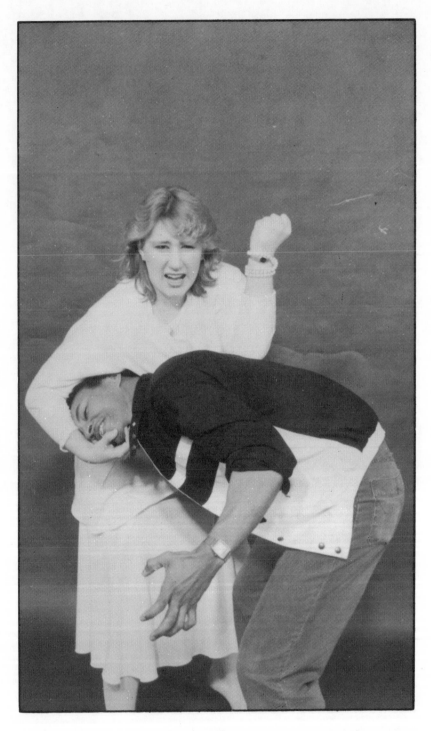

NINE

Combinations 1

Combinations bring your techniques together in one
flurry of activity. The impulse to perform these
techniques as fast as you can should be avoided.
If all your concentration is centered on speed it
could mean a loss of power. Doing the technique
too fast, allows your thought process to pull the
initial strike before full contact is made to the
target area. At the same time, your second strike
is not in a true state of preparedness before its
execution, resulting in a combination, do each
technique with as much power as possible and
complete that technique. The first blow may not
drop your attacker, but if it is executed properly,
it should stun him long enough for you to follow up
with your next technique.

COMBINATION 1

Your attacker has you by the throat as shown. Execute the same release as described for technique number one in Chapter 8. In the next photo you will notice the hands of the attacker have slid off the victim's neck. Slide out of his grasp with your shoulders to completely free yourself and adminster a hammer fist to the groin as shown in the next photo. Turn and run screaming Fire! Fire! Notice how our victim has avoided the hands and feet of her attacker.

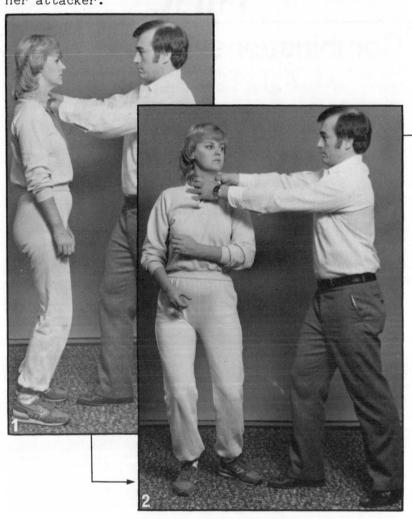

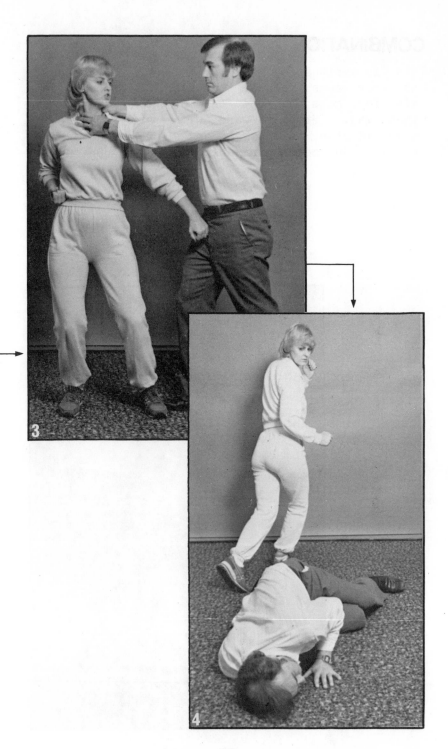

COMBINATION 2

This is a situation many women fear. Your attacker has your arms locked. Step back as shown. Your left leg goes to the outside of your attacker's right leg. Step forward with your right leg as shown in the next photo and grab your attacker's groin. Squeeze, then yank down as you continue to squeeze.

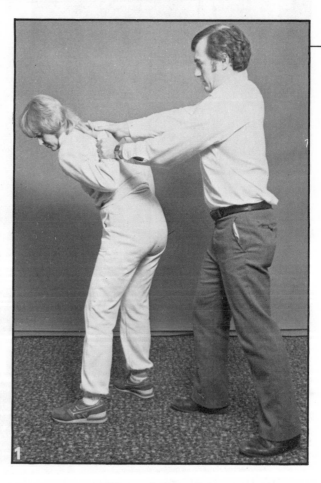

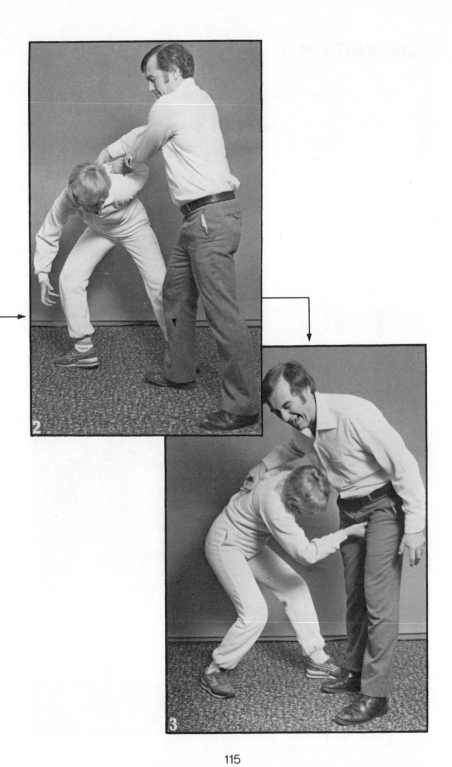

COMBINATION 3

Sometimes when you are grabbed, you are not in a position to execute a knee strike to the groin. The area you have to work in, may be too confining for effective execution of a technique. Reach up and place your palm heel on the nose of your attacker as shown. At the same time, reach behind your attacker's head and grab a hand full of hair. (To grab hair, run your fingers along the scalp and make a fist.) Pull toward you with a hand full of hair and jerk away from yourself with the palm against the face. Execute the last technique with a quick jerk.

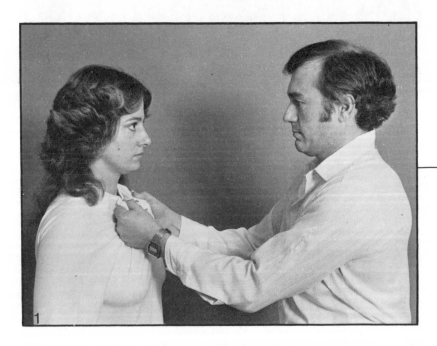

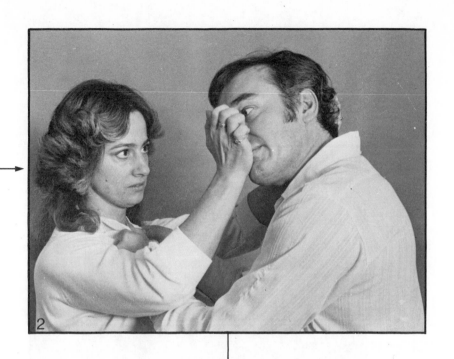

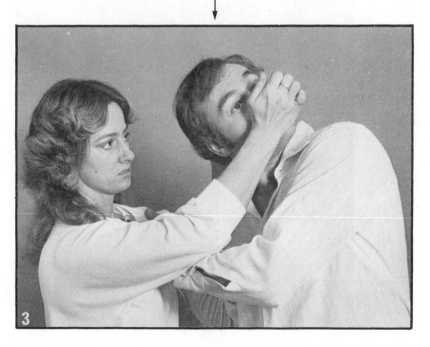

COMBINATION 4

Your attacker has both his hands on your wirst. The
release is the same as in Chapter 6, (two hands
grabbed by one). As soon as your hand is free,
strike with your finger to the eye as shown.
Follow up with a front kick to the groin.

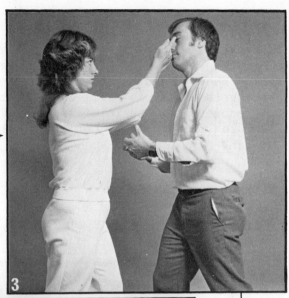

COMBINATION 5

Your attacker reaches out to grab you. Block with a middle block and follow up immediately with a palm heel thrust to the nose. While your attacker's head is still back, or he is attempting to recover from the initial strike, execute a front kick to the groin. Get out of there as quick as you can.

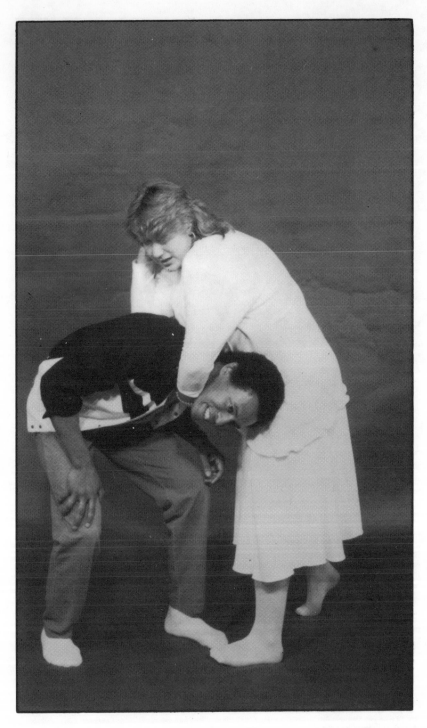

TEN

Combinations 2

The combinations of Chapter 10 are a little more difficult than those of the last chapter. By now, you should be realizing there is no end to the combinations you can invent for yourself with the tools you have. Keep in mind, what you learn from this book should only be a beginning and not an end in itself.

COMBINATION 1

The attacker has grabbed his victim and is threatening to slap her across the face. Execute your release immediately toward the thumb as shown. The release is exactly the same release that you learned in Chapter 6. Follow up on your release with a back fist to the temple of your attacker. Twist around, paying special attention to the movement of your feet. Execute a hammer to the groin. Run away, screaming Fire! Fire!

COMBINATION 2

Your attacker has grabbed you by the shoulder. Turn as shown and continue the movement until your attacker is leaning over, notice the stiffness of the victim's arm and how it is applying pressure to the attacker's elbow. Execute a palm heel to the kidney as shown. When your attacker drops to the ground execute a heel stomp to the groin or another vulnerable area. Remember to keep away from his feet and hands.

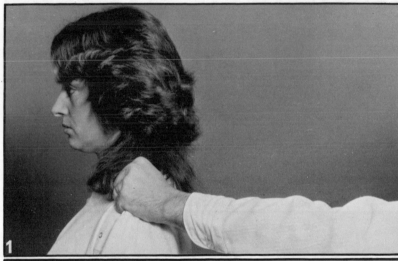

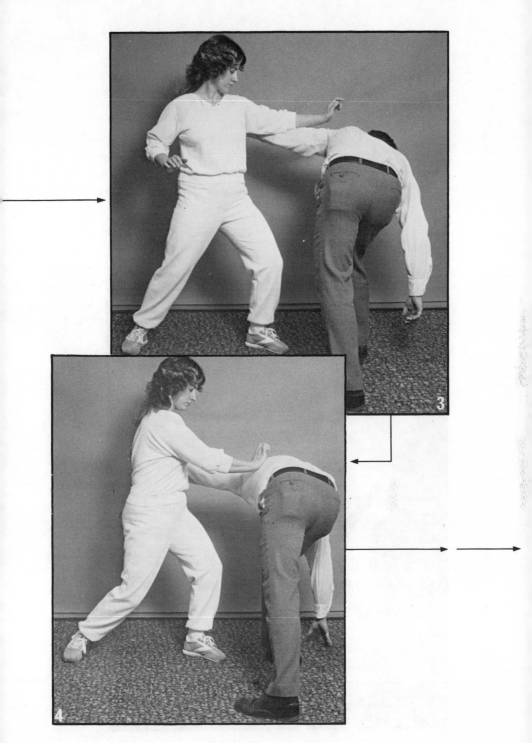

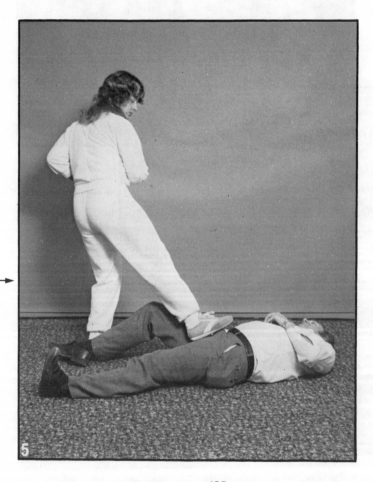

COMBINATION 3

Your attacker has you by the throat with his right hand. Place your left hand directly over the back of the attacker's hand. At the same time, slam your right hand into the crook of his elbow. You may have to execute a diversionary kick here. Step under your attacker's arm keeping a firm hold on his right hand. Continue on through. The last photo shows how to grab the top of the attacker's elbow, pushing down hard and thereby trapping his hand.

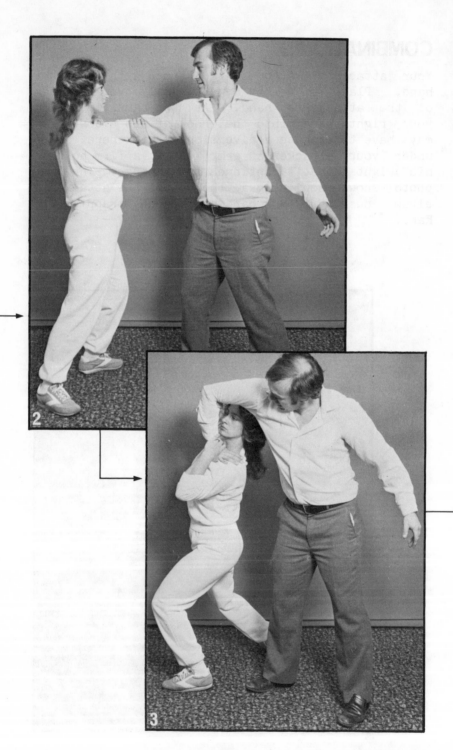

COMBINATION 4

Your attacker has his right hand on your throat and has grabbed your left hand. First release your right hand and while you are doing that simultaneously execute a finger strike to the eye and a knee strike to the groin. Utilize the fact that your attacker is bent over by immediately delivering an elbow smash to his spine. Once he is on the ground drive your heel kick to a vulnerable area, such as a kidney or the spine. Remember to stay away from his hands.

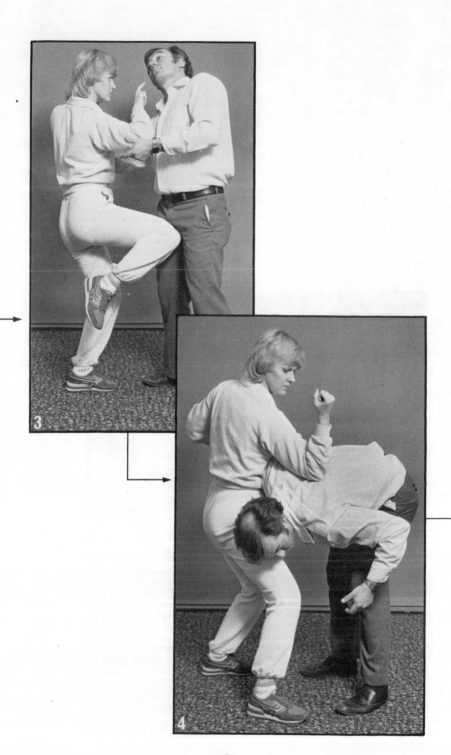

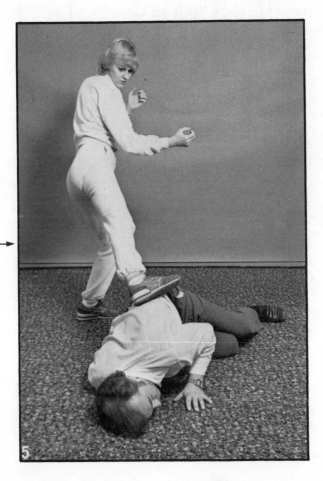

ELEVEN

Weapons

For this, the last phase of your physical training, it is a natural process to move on to weapons. Many of the moves you have been executing will apply to weapon techniques. The only difference of course, you will now be striking with a weapon. The question arises however, what constitutes a weapon? Too many times, individuals think of weapons as only those manufactured. They believe for a weapon to be a weapon it has to have several hundred years tradition. If you compare weapons of long ago to weapons of today, you realize that there is no comparison. Weapons today are too devastating. The present ninja fad, because of movies, is naively considered to be the ultimate in the use of weapons. When ninja were a force in Japan, several ninja would go into a village and probably kill a few people before they left. Today, a handful of soldiers can go into a village and destroy everything, buildings and people, within a few minutes.

For your purpose of self defense, neither guns, nor swords are practical for every day use, so what constiutes a weapon? Anything, you can get your hands on that is solid enough to strike without breaking, light enough to swing easily and heavy enough to cause damage. An ashtray, the telephone, car keys, a pen, the list can be endless. Make a list and familiarize yourself with these weapons. Practice with them. If you have an ashtray in your right hand, practice blocking your partner with your left hand and **striking** at a vulnerable area with the ashtray. Work on different techniques with different objects.

Holding a long stick

Hands are natural, approximately eight inches apart. Your thumb and index finger are reasonably loose, the remaining three fingers are firmly gripped on your weapon. This gives your wrists freedom to snap your weapon when you strike. When changing hands to accomodate a circular movement with your weapon and you are swinging from left to right over your head, your left hand slides over top of your right hand as you swing. When contact is made, both hands must be firm on the weapon.

COMBINATION 1

Your attacker is coming for you. (Notice the reverse grip the victim has on the weapon, as well as the foot stance.) Thrust the weapon as hard as you can into the stomach or solar plexus of your attacker. As you do this, try to time the strike with the motion of your body. Get your full weight into your strike. Swing the weapon down, around and over your right shoulder and strike the head as shown. Notice the change of the hand position.

COMBINATION 2

Combination number two is identical to Combination number one with the exception of swinging the weapon. Instead of swinging the weapon around and over your head, swing it in the opposite direction. Notice that the left hand has changed position in the last photo.

COMBINATION 3

Your attacker attempts to grab you from the rear. (If he has managed to grab you, you can still administer this technique.) Pay close attention to your foot movement in this technique. Notice that the victim has begun to turn and while turning has shifted her hands for a more solid strike. In the last photo notice the position of the right foot, the victim executes a strike to the side of the attacker's head.

142

COMBINATION 4

This is a combination of the previous techniques learned, executed against two attackers. In the first photo the victim jabs the weapon into the midsection of the first attacker immediately jabbing the weapon into the front attacker. The victim then executes Combination number one and Combination number three.

144

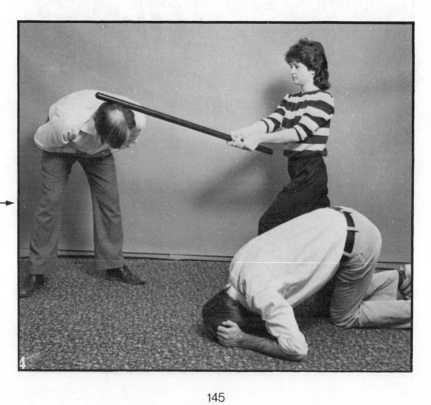

146

TWELVE

Survival Defense

WOMEN ALONE

At home

(1) Your door should be equipped with a door viewer and deadbolt lock with a one inch throw.

(2) All windows should be secure. Draw window shades or drapes after dark.

(3) All entrances and garages should be well lit.

(4) Never remain alone in an apartment laundry room, mailroom or parking garage.

(5) Avoid feminine identification. Do not put your first name on your mailbox or in the telephone book. Use two initials and your last name.

(6) Unknown persons should not be admitted to your premises unless proper credentials are presented.

(7) Should a stranger request use of your phone, do not allow the person to enter. Offer to make the call yourself.

(8) Should you return home to find windows and

doors tampered with DO NOT ENTER OR CALL OUT! Go to a neighbour and call the police.

On the street

(1) Plan your route and avoid short cuts through parks, vacant lots or unlit areas.

(2) Do not overburden yourself with packages and a bulky purse.

(3) Walk near the curb and away from alleys and doorways.

(4) If you suspect you are being followed, cross the street; go to the nearest home, service station or open business premises and call the police.

Public transportation

(1) Try to avoid isolated bus stops.

(2) Sit near other women or near the driver.

(3) If someone bothers you tell the driver immediately.

Hitchhicking

Police implore women not to hitchhike under any circumstances.

In you car

(1) Always lock your car when entering and leaving it.

(2) View the interior of your vehicle before entering to assure that nobody is hiding inside. Do this even if the doors were locked.

(3) Have your keys in hand so you do not have to linger before entering your car.

(4) Travel on well lit streets and keep your purse out of sight.

(5) If you have car trouble in a dark area, raise the hood of the car, lock yourself in and wait for the police to arrive. If a stranger offers to help, do not get out of your car. Ask the person to call for assistance.

(6) If you suspect someone is following you, drive to the nearest service station, drive-in restaurant, police station and blow the horn.

Public places

Use caution in conversations with stangers. Avoid giving your name, address or place of employment. In theatres, avoid dark corners and sit near the aisle.

Purse snatching

Do not carry large sums of money in your purse. If possible carry a small purse hidden from view under your arm. Be wary of approaching strangers. If someone grabs your purse do not resist.

Babysitting

Leave information with your family about babysitting location, phone number and the time you can be expected home. Once inside the house lock all the windows and doors. Be escorted home after dark.

THIRTEEN

Victims Role!

Many victims of rape experience fear, depression, guilt, loss of normal functioning sex lives and lack of confidence and trust. All these feelings are normal and it is vital to realize that you are not alone with these feelings. Understanding the stress and coping with the aftermath of a sexual assault, is all part of the self defense procedure. Realizing rape is not a sexual act, but a violent one, is the first step. Laws have now been changed to categorize rape as assault with better protection for the victim. Sexual assault laws are outlined in the Criminal Code in Chapter 14.

Realize the importance of reporting the crime directed against you, obtaining justice against your attacker, possibly preventing him from directing more violence against you or some other woman. In reporting this crime, you should realize that such a report will institute an investigation by the police. Procedures must be followed and this Chapter is to help you understand the kind of things you will be asked to go through. None of these procedures are directed at you personally but are all part of legislation guidelines directed by the government. As an individual you have the right to understand each procedure undergone during the entire process. If you have any questions at any time do not hesitate to ask the person looking after you.

Once you have made your report to the police, they are required by law to investigate your report. A statement will be taken from you to establish what has taken place. The police will also want to know where the offence occurred, so evidence can be sought out. They will be looking for possible fingerprints, weapons, stains or other clues as to the identity of your assailant. Do not touch or remove anything. Something that may appear insignificant to you could be of great value to the police.

Medical process

As soon as possible after the asault, see a physician. Only a doctor can determine if you have injuries, either external or internal and administer the correct treatment. The physician can also advise you regarding tests for sexually transmitted diseases and / or pregnancy. He will take the necessary blood samples and smears so that a laboratory can check for various diseases. For your own well being, you must follow your physician's advice. If you have not been protected by a birth control method, speak to your doctor and if your are concerned about becoming pregnant he can tell you the various options available to you.

DO NOT bathe, shower or douche. These actions can destroy evidence. However, if you have done so, it is still important to have a physical examination and take the necessary tests for sexually transmitted diseases.

A physician will check for any signs of bruises or lacerations on your body. A pelvic examination will also be done. Your genital area will be examined for tears, cuts, bruises or any other signs that force was used.

Samples will be taken from your vagina to check for the presence of sperm and semen. The presence of moving sperm will help to determine when you last had sexual intercourse.

Several other tests may be performed while you are being examined.

Fingernail scrapings. If you scratched your assailant or tore at his clothing you may have material under your fingernails that will help to identify him.

Pubic hair examination. Combings of your pubic area may reveal hairs from your assailant. These hairs may be used to help identify him by the Center of Forensic Sciences.

Woods lamp examination. This lamp causes semen to glow in a dark room. This helps the physician to pinpoint areas of your body or clothing that should be examined for specimens.

Police investigation

An interview with the investigating officer will probably take place after you have made your initial report and this will be the most important phase of the investigation. Your ability to recall the details of the incident is essential.

You will be asked about the force and threats the suspect used, if he frightened or threatened you, as well as any weapon he may have used or threatened to use. You will also be asked to tell what if anything you said or did to resist the suspect. These details are most important because it is necessary in court to prove that you did not agree to the sexual act.

Be as candid and precise as possible. Do not leave out any details, even if you feel they may tend to weaken your account. If these details are not known now and come out later in the trail it could discredit your testimony. Many questions may be embarrassing and may seem very trivial. But all the details of the incident will assist in the investigation.

Feel free at any time to ask the investigating officer any questions about the investigation, court process, or anything else you wish to know. If injuries such as cuts and bruises occurred during the incident, these should be reported. The officer may ask that photographs be taken of these injuries. Pictures can be extremely important in a trial long after the injuries have healed. You do not have to agree to have these pictures taken but this kind of evidence can be very helpful to your case.

After a suspect has been arrested, you may be asked to look at the man in a police line-up. You will be asked to concentrate on each man and compare him to the others. You can have the men do or say something specific to help with your identification if need be.

If the suspect is released on bail on his own promise (personal recognizance), he will be instructed to not talk to you or see you at any time in any way. If he does contact you, report the circumstances to the investigating officer immediately.

Court procedures

Many sexual assault cases do not involve a trail since the offender can not be found or there is insufficient evidence with which to charge a suspect. However, in the event that your case does get to trail the following information will be helpful.

Before you appear in court you will probably be interviewed by the Crown Attorney assigned to your case. During the interview you will be asked to review the details of the incident. Sometimes the Crown will not proceed with the charges. If this happens to you ask the Crown Attorney why this decision was made. You have the right to know the reasons why your case will not go to court.

Canada has new laws that limit what can be brought out about your background and any previous sexual experiences you might have had with other men. We cover this law in the next chapter.

Again if there are words or procedures you do not understand, ask for an explanation. Make sure you have a name and telephone number to call in case you have additional information to give or questions to ask about your case. If the accused's defense lawyer should contact you to discuss the case, ask the Crown Attorney what you should do or say.

It is possible that a preliminary hearing will be held in an open court before a judge. The accused and his lawyer will be present. If your testimony is required, you will probably be asked to describe the incident. The defense lawyer will have the right to question you about details. At the end of the preliminary hearing the judge reviews the evidence present. If he determines that there is evidence which is sufficient in law to constitute the crime of rape, the case will be referred to trail. If the judge does not find such evidence, the case will be dismissed.

You should ask the Crown Attorney which type of hearings will occur and if you will be required to attend. A supoena will be issued if you must testify. The Crown Attorney will explain the various procedures to you and tell you about your role. If words are used that are unfamiliar to you, be sure to ask questions. You have a right to know and understand what is happening at each stage.

It is not easy to testify but it is not as difficult as television and movies make it appear to be. The Crown Attorney will ask simple question, knowing what your answers will be. Your job is to tell the truth as clearly as you can. If you don't understand a question, ask for an explanation or a rewording. Even though it may be difficult or painful for you to talk about the details of the incident, it is necessary for you to testify if the accused is to be found guilty.

When you have completed your testimony, you will be allowed to stay in the courtroom and watch the rest of the trail. If something happens that you think you can clarify, make sure that you mention it to the Crown Attorney at the next break. The accused does not have to testify and if he does, it will not be held against him. All reasonable doubt must be erased from the minds of the jurors or judge through the evidence presented. A finding of not guilty does not mean that the accused did not commit the crime or that you have not told the truth. It may simply mean that there was not enough evidence for the jury or judge to believe beyond a reasonable doubt that the accused was guilty.

Victim services

There may be people in your area who have worked with sexual assault victims and who are available to help you. In some areas there are rape crisis hotlines that you can call to talk to someone who will understand how you are feeling and be able to give you advice about medical and legal information available to you. Having someone with whom you can talk and who will be able to answer your questions about reporting the incident might make you feel more comfortable.

If you do not know of a place to go for help, ask the attending physician, the investigating officer or the Crown Attorney for information. You might also contact a mental health clinic in your area for suggestions. Because sexual assault is a painful and upsetting experience it is important that you receive understanding, care and support from those around you during this time.

FOURTEEN

The Law!

BILL C-127

Bill C-127 makes substantive amendments to the Criminal Code in the areas of assault offences, sexual assault offences and child abduction. In addition, certain evidentiary rules employed in sexual assault trials are modified and certain offences are made sex neutral, that is to say certain provisions of the criminal law will apply equally to men and women.

Background

Bill C-127 traces its roots to 1978 and the Law Reform Commission's Report on sexual offences. The report proposed a sweeping reform of the law on sexual offences. All aspects of the criminal law in this area were to be justified on one or more of the three grounds.

(1) Protection of the individual integrity of the person from non-consensual sexual contact.

(2) Protection of children and the psychologically vulnerable from sexual contact.

(3) Protection of public decency; the right not to

have one's sexual values offended in public.

On January 12th, 1981, Bill C-53 was given first reading in the House of Commons. The Bill carried forward the basic recommendations of the Law Reform Commission with respect to sexual assault and sexual conduct with children. In addition, it proposed the repeal of the 'public morality office' of buggery and bestiality as well as reform of gross indecency. The Bill also propsed to deal with child pornography and child abduction. The Bill was given second reading on December 17th, 1981 and referred to the Standing Committee or Justice and Legal Affairs.

Due to the inability of Committee members to agree on the provisions of the Bill dealing with child pornography, the Committee agreed it would consider only the assault, sexual assault and child abduction parts of Bill C-53.

As a result, Bill C-127 was introduced, comprised of the amendment to the Criminal code that had received the approval of the Justice and Legal Affairs Committee and was passed by the House of Commons on August 4th, 1982.

Highlights of BILL C-127

The amendments to the Criminal Code contained in Bill C-127 can be divided into six general areas dealing with assault offences, sexual assualt offences, evidence in sexual assault cases, the degenderizing of certain offences, child abduction and consequential amendments.

Assault

Bill C-127 proposes a three tiered structure of assault offences. The former offences of common assault, assault causing bodily harm and unlawfully causing bodily harm are repealed. The assault and sexual assault offences proposed by the Bill are enacted as Part VI of the Criminal Code, 'Offences against the person and reputation'. The new Section 244 describes the necessary elements of assault.

(1) The intentional direct or indirect application of force to another person without that person's consent, or

(2) An attempt or threat by act or gesture, to apply force to another person when one has present ability to do so or causes the other person to believe that one has present abiltity to do so, or

(3) Accosting or impeding another person or begging while wearing or carrying a weapon or an imitation of a weapon.

This definition of assault expressly applies to all forms of assault, including sexual assault.

Section 244(3) outlines the circumstances where no consent to the assault or sexual assault is obtained. It provides that no consent is obtained where the complainant submits or does not resist by reason of:

(1) The application of force to the complainant or to a third party.

(2) The threat or fear of the application of force to the complainant or a third party.

(3) Fraud.

(4) The exercise of authority.

Section 244(4) provides for the defense of mistaken belief as to consent. This will be discussed in the context of sexual assault offences.

Three levels of assault offences will be provided by the Criminal code. The first level offence,

Section 245, known simply as 'assault', is a hybrid offence punishable either by summary conviction or by a maximum of five years imprisonment on indictment. An immediate effect will be to permit police officers to arrest battering husbands where they have not in fact witnessed the assault. Section 245.1 is the second level of assault, 'assault with a weapon' or 'causing bodily harm'. Where in the commission of an assault the offender carries, uses or threatens to use a weapon or an imitation of a weapon or where he causes bodily harm to the complainant he is guilty of an indictable offence with a maximum penalty of ten years imprisonment.

'Bodily harm' is defined by Section 245.1(2) as any hurt or injury to the complainant that interferes with his or her health or comfort and that is more that merely transient or trifling in nature. The most serious assault offence is agravated assault. Section 245.2 provides that where the offender wounds, maims, disfigures or endangers the life of the complainant he has committed an aggravated assault and is subject to a maximum penalty of up to 14 years imprisonment.

The offences of assault causing bodily harm and unlawfully causing bodily harm contained in Section 245(2) are repealed. The new second level assault offence, Section 245.1 will provide for the offence causing bodily harm and Section 245.3 provides for the offence of unlawfully causing bodily harm with a maximum penalty of up to 10 years imprisonment.

The offence of assault with intent to commit an indictable offence (Section 246) is repealed and is not reenacted. Because assault can be proceeded with by way of indictment pursuant to the new Section 245 there is no need for this specific offence.

The offence of assault on a peace officer engaged in the execution of his duty is retained and has been renumbered Section 246.

The current Section 228, to wound, maim, disfigure, endanger life or prevent arrest, with intent to cause bodily harm or involving the discharge of a firearm is amended. The new Section 228 includes only the reference to discharging a firearm with intent to wound, maim, disfigure, endanger the life or prevent the arrest of anyone and carries a maximum penalty of 14 years imprisonment.

SEX ASSAULT

The most significant change of Bill C-127 is the revision of the substantive law of sexual offences including the abolishment of the offences of rape and indecent assault.

Rape occurred when a man had sexual intercourse with a woman who was not his wife, without her consent. The maximum punishment was life imprisonment. The offence of indecent assault differed depending on the sex of the victim. A person of either sex could commit an indecent assault on a female, however, only a male could indecently assault another male. Indecent assault was not defined but included sexual assaults in which sexual intercourse was not involved. These offenses were included in Part IV of the Criminal Code, 'Sexual Offences, Public Morals and Disorderly Conduct'.

Bill C-127 radically changes the substantive law of sexual offences. These offences will be included in Part VI of the Criminal Code 'Offences against the person and reputation'. Section 244, described above, which sets out the elements of assault is also applicable to sexual assaults.

Bill C-127 provides for a three tiered structure of sexual assaults. Sexual assault would be made a hybrid offence by Section 246.1. It is not defined and would be punishable either on indictment by a maximum of 10 years imprisonment or on summary conviction. The second level of sexual assault, indictable and punishable by a maximum of 14 years imprisonment would occur where a weapon or imitation weapon is carried, used or threatened to be used; where there is a threat of bodily harm to a third party; where bodily harm is caused to the complainant or where there is more than one party to the assault. Thus, where several persons sexually assault a complainant they can be charged with this second level offence. Aggravated sexual assault, the most serious sexual assault offence, occurs where a sexual assault is accompanied by wounding, maiming, disfiguring or endangering the life of the complainant. The maximum punishment is life imprisonment.

The new Section 244 sets out in subsection 3 the factors which vitiate consent to any form of assault, including the application of force to the complainant or thrid party, fraud, threats of force and the exercise of authority.

Where an accused is charged with an offence under Sections 246.1, 246.2 or 246.3 in respect of a complainant under 14 years of age, Section 246.1(2) provides that the consent of that complainant is not a defence unless the accused is less than three years older than the complainant. Therefore, if the accused, aged 18 is charged with sexual assault in respect of a 13 year old complainant, the fact that the complainant consented to the conduct is not a defense to the charge. However, if the accused were 15 years of age, the consent of a 13 year old complainant would be a defense to the charge.

Section 246.8 expressly states that a husband or wife may be charged with a sexual assault offence whether or not the spouses were living together at the time of the sexual assault. The emphasis of the new provisions is on the violent nature of sexual assault other than on its sexual nature.

This is why such conduct is treated as a subset of the general assault provisions rather than as a special category of criminal conduct.

The conduct of a sexual assault trail

The Criminal Code was amended in 1976 to repeal a provision requiring corroboration in certain sexual offence prosecutions such as rape and indecent assault. There has been some doubt whether that amendment had the desired effect and accordingly, Bill C-127 expressly sites that corroboration is not required for a conviction for sexual assault. Furthermore, Section 139 of the Criminal Code which required corroboration for other sexual offences, such as incest, is repealed. In addition, the judge cannot instruct the jury that it is unsafe to find an accused guilty of these offences in the absence of corroboration.

Recent complaint rule abrogated

At common law there existed an exception to the hearsay rule which permitted a complainant to give evidence of a 'complaint' as to a sexual offence. To be admissable the complaint must have been made at the first reasonable opportunity after the alleged offence and it must not have been elicited by leading questions. The defense could offer evidence of the lack of a complaint or the lapse of time between the attack and the complaint as adversely reflecting upon the complainant's testimony. Bill C-127 provides, in Section 246.5 that the rules regarding recent complaint in sexual assault cases are abrogated. The ordinary rules of evidence which are applicable to all criminal offences will govern.

Sexual conduct of the complainant

The former Section 142 of the Criminal Code provided that in respect of the offences of rape, attempted rape, sexual intercourse with a female under 14 or indecent assault on a female, no question could be asked as to the complainant's conduct with someone other than the accused unless a judge, at an in camera hearing decided that:

The weight of the evidence is such that to exclude it would prevent the making of a just determination of fact in the proceedings, including the credibility of the complainant.

In addition, Section 142 prescribed the procedure to be followed when such evidence was desired to be introduced. In June 1980, the Supreme Court of Canada in the R. V. Forsythe decision held that a complainant was a compellable witness at the in camera hearing and in that context her evidence was rebuttable. The decision was criticised by many who felt that any inquiry into past sexual conduct should be prohibited.

Bill C-127 replaces Section 142 with Section 246.6 dealing with the three new sexual assault offences. The provisions with respect to giving notice and particulars of the evidence sought and forbidding publication are essentially the same. However, the criteria for the admission of evidence of previous sexual conduct with someone other than the accused are narrowed to three.

(1) Evidence that rebuts evidence of the complainant's sexual activity or absence thereof that was previously introduced by the prosecution.

(2) Evidence of specific instances of the complainant's sexual activity tending to establish the identity of the person who had sexual contact with the complainant on the occasion set out in the charge.

(3) Evidence of sexual activity that took place on the same occasion as the sexual activity that forms the subject matter of the charge, where the evidence relates to the consent that the accused

alleges he believes was given by the complainant.

The first ground is straight forward, if the prosecution wishes to avoid such questioning it need only refrain from raising the issue.

The second ground, dealing with the establishment of identity, is intended to govern cases in which the accused contends that he did not have sexual contact with the complainant at all and wishes to prove from some physical evidence, such as the presence of semen, or blood, that some other person was responsible.

The third ground, dealing with evidence of sexual activity that took place on the same occasion as that raised in the charge is intended to govern situations in which a complainant is alleged to have had sexual contact with more than one person on one occasion and the accused wishes to allege belief in consent from the complainant's conduct.

In addition, Section 246.6(3) expressly states that the complainant is not a compellable witness at the in camera hearing. A new section, Section 246.7, expressly forbids the admission of evidence of a complainant's sexual reputation to challenge or support his or her credibility.

Honest mistakes to consent

Prior to the amendments contained in Bill C-127 an accused charged with rape could plead the defense of mistake of fact as to the consent of the complainant.

In 1980, the Supreme Court of Canada held in Pappajohn vs. The Queen, that an unreasonable yet honest mistake as to consent could be an effective defense to a charge of rape. Resonableness of mistake was not irrelevant in determining the honesty of the belief but it was not required as a matter of law. The new section, Section 244(B) clarifies and codefies the law with respect to an accused's mistaken belief as to consent. Section 244(4) directs a judge, when satisfied there is sufficient evidence which if believed could constitute a defense based on mistake, to instruct a jury in reviewing the evidence.

'relating to the determination of the honesty of the belief, to consider the presence or absence of reasonable grounds for that belief'

An honest, though unreasonable belief that there was consent will still theoretically be a defense, but the trier of the fact is now bound to consider how reasonable that belief is in determining whether or not it is honestly held.

The degenderizing of offences

Bill C-127 also amends provisions of the Criminal Code to make certain offences equally applicable to men and women. Formerly, rape was defined in such a way that only a man could rape a woman who was not his wife. The sexual assault offences, Sections 246.1, 246.2 and 246.3, can be committed by a male or female against a male or female. In addition, Section 246.8 expressly provides that a spouse can be charged with a sexual assault offence.

The definition of 'prostitute' in Section 179(1) is amended by the Bill to read:

'Prostitute' means a person of either sex who engages in prostitution.

Also, the offence of procuring for the purpose of prostitution in Section 195(1) and (2) as amended by replacing the term 'female person' with the term 'a person'.

Consequential amendments

The amendments to the Criminal Code contained in Bill C-127 require amendments to certain other federal statutes particularly due to the reform of the sexual assault offences.

The Canada Evidence Act, currently retains the common law exception, which allows a spouse to testify against the other spouse in cases involving his or her health or liberty. Thus where a husband assaulted his wife, the wife would be competent and compellable to give evidence against her husband. The amendments to the Canada Evidence Act in Bill C-127 expand the situation where a spouse is a compellable witness. The new section 4(2) provides that where a spouse is charged with certain offences, including contributing to juvenile delinquency, sexual offences, child abduction and bigamy, the spouse is a competent and compellable witness. In addition, Section 4(3.1) provides a young person under 14 years of age, including murder, infanticide, criminal negligence causing death and assault, the other spouse is both competent and compellable. These provisions are intended to assist in prosecution in child abuse cases.

The Divorce Act is amended to replace the reference to 'rape' in Paragraph 3(b) with the term 'has committed an assault involving sexual intercourse'.

The Extradition Act is also amended to refer to the new sexual offences and section references are renumbered in order to correspond with relevant sections of the amended Criminal Code.

The National Defence Act is amended to provide that a service tribunal shall not try cases of murder, manslaughter, sexual assault or child abduction.

FIFTEEN

Myths or Fact?

Sexual assault has for centuries been an emotion charged topic. As a result, numerous myths about the crime have developed and some of these prevailed, obscuring its true nature.

Although founded on misinformation and erroneous assumption, myths are extremely powerful. They influence society's attitudes, beliefs and actions regarding the act, the assailant and especially the victim. They affect the way the laws, police, courts and juries respond. They color the meaning in which families and friends react - too frequently expressing skepticism, rejecting the victims and denying their support, making them feel even more alone and isolated than they do already. Finally (and perhaps this is the most lethal consequence of all), fictions influence the way victims feel about themselves. Since many victims have internalized the prevalent mythology which promotes the idea of the deserving victim, victims often feel damaged, ashamed and guilty for having in some way precipitated the attack.

Those dealing with victims of sexual assault are not immune to the traditional biases of society. It is therefore imperative that the myths be critically examined if intervening agents are to be

171

truly effective. Agents must be aware of the myths and understand that while there may be some truth in some of them for some individual situations, they do not represent the facts.

Myth

Rape is an act motivated by sexual desire.

Fact

Rape is an act of violence and aggression, not sex. Sex is merely the means of assault. As opposed to sexual gratification, the offenders are seeking domination and control by humiliating their victims and forcing them to engage in sexual intercourse against their will.

Myth

Most rapes are reported to the police.

Fact

Most rapes are not reported to the police. While it is impossible to determine the number of rapes not reported, it has been estimated that only 10 percent are reported to the police.

Myth

Most rapes occur in dark alleys.

Fact

At least half of all rapes occur in a residence, the single most common place (about one third) being the homes of the victims. Rape also occurs in more 'dangerous' places like deserted streets, parks, alleys and underground garages.

Myth

Rape happens only when it is dark.

Fact

Rape can occur at any time. Peak hours are however, between 8:00 p.m. and 2:00 a.m.

Myth

If a woman resists, she cannot be raped.

Fact
This myth confuses consent with submission. According to a study conducted by Menachem Amir, force is absent in only 15 percent of incidents. These usually involve child rapes.

Myth
Only certain kinds of women get raped.

Fact
Rape can happen to any woman, regardless of her age, physical appearance or character. Six month old infants as well as 73 year old women have been victims of this crime.

Myth
Women who are raped are 'asking for it'!

Fact
It is the rapists who are responsible for the rape, not the victims.

Myth
A rape victim will be battered, burised and hysterical.

Fact
Most rape victims are not visibly physically injured. Often threats of violence are sufficient to cause women to submit.

Myth
Women secretly desire to be raped.

Fact
It is difficult for anyone to seriously believe that people have a desire to be assaulted, sexually or in any other way. Almost everyone wishes to have a healthy relationship with another person and the use of force or pain can hardly be called healthy.

Myth

Women frequently cry 'rape' falsely for reasons of revenge, pregnancy, etc.

Fact

The incidence of false accusations of rape appears to be equal to the false accusations of any other crime.

Myth

The rapist is acting on an uncontrollable sexual impulse.

Fact

Men can control their sexual desires or find outlets for them which do not involve assaulting another person. The fact that most rapes are premeditated and are not the result of an impulse is shown by Amir's investigation, 58 per cent of single, 73 per cent of pair and 90 per cent of group rapes are planned in advance.

Myth

Rapists are insane.

Fact

I most cases rapists do not suffer from mental illness. A 1965 study conducted by Amir revealed that, with the exception of 3 per cent of them, rapists have normal sexual personalities. The only area in which they differ is in their tendency to express anger and violence openly.

Myth

The rapist is a stranger to his victim.

Fact

In over 50 percent of reported incidents of rape the offenders are known is some capacity to their victims.

Assisting the victims of sexual assault depends in part upon the ability to separate the popular

fictions from the realities of the act. But myths
die hard, especially when they are imbedded in
beliefs, attitudes and values which are socially
learned.

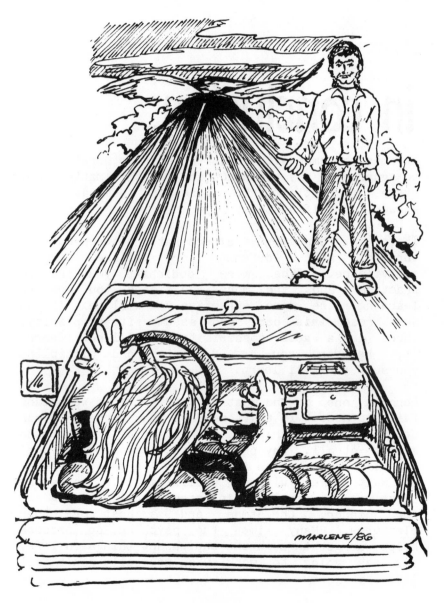

in conclusion...

It must be emphasized that there is no surefire way to guarantee any technique, or for that matter, any style of martial art. None of them are 'the' answer for self defense.

There is, however, a direct ratio between success through self defense or failure through ambivilance. The more dedicated you are to practice and the more dediciated you are to learning, the more effective you will be. If you just read this book and assume its simplicity, there is a good possibility you will not learn. If, however, you are dedicated and discipline yourself you will learn.

Perhaps one of the most difficult things we humans fail to accept is that one day, what happend to our neighbour could happen to us. The secret is no secret at all. Any professional learns to 'psyche' himself up. We as individuals 'psyche' ourselves up many times without realizing it. We psyche ourselves up for an anticipated vacation, going out for dinner, Christmas and a host of other pleasures. Many times the psyching up process helps us get through the unpleasant things in life, such as going to work when we really don't feel like it.

The best way to approach your training method is to make it as pleasurable as possible. Look forward to learning these methods well. Set a certain time aside every other day and pamper yourself. Pamper yourself for you, you can do it and you deserve to learn. Good luck!

The authors

Both Bill Daniels and Sharon van Dyk have been involved in the martial arts for several years and are of course both black belts.

Bill Daniels has a writing background having done work for newspapers, magazines and radio as well as editing a martial arts magazine. He also had experience being a free lance photo journalist.

Bill's martial arts training began the same time as his journalism career and the two went together very nicely, affording many opportunities to write about the martial arts and its many styles.

Bill is presently working towards his 4th degree in Hapkido as well as teaching at his own club in Belleville, Ontario.

Sharon van Dyk began training in Karate, Kung Fu and Ju Jitsu in 1974 and received her black belt (shodan) in June 1979.

Sharon has lectured for several years, teaching a self defense course at various educational institutes and interested organizations. Sharon joined Belleville martial arts academy in 1983 as an instructor.

Sharon also designed, developed and instructed an extensive course for women in the art of self defense. She continues to lecture, instruct and is now working on a second martial arts book specifically designed for school age children.